Advance Praise for

BEYOND DISTRACTION

"*Beyond Distraction: Five Practical Ways to Focus the Mind* offers a comprehensive map for accomplishing the inviting promise of the title. Shaila Catherine draws on her deep reservoir of meditative experience and her careful study of the Buddha's teachings to highlight many of the familiar obstacles in meditation practice and how best to successfully overcome them. This book contains a wealth of pragmatic advice for both new and experienced meditators, and it will be an invaluable guide for all those journeying on the path to greater freedom."
—Joseph Goldstein, author of *Mindfulness: A Practical Guide to Awakening*

"Shaila is a master of the mind. She brings deep wisdom from decades of personal practice and teaching together with accessible and pragmatic tools in a user-friendly format. Whether you are just beginning to meditate or have logged many hours on the cushion, this book is for you."
—Judson Brewer, author of *The Craving Mind*

"This book encourages us to understand our minds better, and to trust that we can shift from drivenness toward a gentler, more intentional way of living. Lots of helpful advice for these times, marked by anxiety and uncertainty!"
—Kate Lila Wheeler, editor of *The State of Mind Called Beautiful*

"This is one of the most detailed and comprehensive guides to meditation out there. Deeply rooted in the Dharma but easy to follow, this very practical book will transform your ability to meditate, so you can transform your mind."
—Kristin Neff, author of *Fierce Self-Compassion*

T0000975

"*Beyond Distraction* offers readers a treasure trove of practices to live a fulfilled life, free from the division of focused versus distracted. Shaila points out the myriad expressions of distraction—such as daydreams, fantasies, and projections. She then offers skillful means to dissolve the notion of distraction and to engage fully with our priorities. Readable, clear, and down-to-earth, *Beyond Distraction* deserves a wide readership."
—Christopher Titmuss, author of *The Buddha of Love* and *The Spiritual Roots of Mindfulness*

"An excellent, entirely approachable, and eminently practical companion on the path of cultivation from one of America's most beloved Buddhist teachers. Shaila Catherine has that rare combination of extensive understanding of Theravada Buddhist philosophy and decades teaching vipassana and jhāna to Buddhist meditation practitioners in Silicon Valley. If you seek an exceptional guide for developing wisdom, compassion, and freedom from suffering—on the cushion and in daily life—look no further."
—Lisa Dale Miller, author of *Effortless Mindfulness*

"In this thorough and useful book, Shaila Catherine translates ancient Buddhist wisdom into practical explanations and exercises to help us work with our distracted minds. Her clear instructions and wise suggestions will help the reader to no longer be at the mercy of their thoughts and to find deeper places of joy and freedom."
—Diana Winston, author of *The Little Book of Being*

Beyond Distraction

Five Practical Ways to Focus the Mind

SHAILA CATHERINE

Wisdom Publications
199 Elm Street
Somerville, MA 02144 USA
wisdomexperience.org

Library of Congress Cataloging-in-Publication Data
Names: Catherine, Shaila, author.
Title: Beyond distraction: five practical ways to focus the mind /
    Shaila Catherine.
Description: First. | Somerville: Wisdom Publications, 2022. |
    Includes bibliographical references and index.
Identifiers: LCCN 2021046134 (print) | LCCN 2021046135 (ebook) |
    ISBN 9781614297871 (paperback) | ISBN 9781614298113 (ebook)
Subjects: LCSH: Attention—Religious aspects—Buddhism.
Classification: LCC BQ7805 .C38 2022 (print) | LCC BQ7805 (ebook) |
    DDC 294.3/444—dc23/eng/20220120
LC record available at https://lccn.loc.gov/2021046134
LC ebook record available at https://lccn.loc.gov/2021046135

ISBN 978-1-61429-787-1   ebook ISBN 978-1-61429-811-3

26 25 24 23
5 4 3 2

Cover design by Phil Pascuzzo. Interior design by Tony Lulek.

Please visit fscus.org.

CONTENTS

INTRODUCTION

Lost in Thought

THE HUMAN MIND is a wonderful asset, capable of composing poetry, mapping DNA sequences, contemplating causality, developing the theory of relativity, and putting a human on the moon.

While we might not all have the intellectual aptitude of an Einstein, we each possess a resilient mind that can observe, communicate, investigate, problem-solve, and plan. Our minds can quickly process complicated information that we can consciously use to shape how we experience our lives.

Thinking is certainly useful, but the untrained mind may tend toward repeating distressing patterns. Many people suffer from chronic comparing, endless worrying, seductive fantasizing, or relentless planning. People can even develop anxiety through countless hours obsessing about the past or imaginative rehearsals of how they might respond to encounters in the future.

The Buddha declared, "I do not see even one other thing that, when untamed, unguarded, unprotected, and unrestrained, leads to such great harm as the mind. The mind, when untamed, unguarded, unprotected, and unrestrained, leads to great harm."

The good news is that we can purposely choose to train our minds to let go of unskillful thought habits. As the Buddha concluded, "I do not see even one other thing that, when tamed, guarded, protected, and restrained, leads to such great good as the mind. The mind, when tamed, guarded, protected, and restrained, leads to great good."[1]

In meditation retreats, classes, and study groups, I have taught the sequence outlined in this book as a methodical process for removing distracting thoughts. This practice is designed to dispel thoughts that divert meditators from maintaining focus on their meditation objects or present experiences. These strategies can augment a wide range of meditation practices and can be combined with practices of mindfulness, loving-kindness and compassion, concentration, and insight.

The training begins by recognizing that a thought is just that—a thought, a creation of our own minds. From this recognition, we distinguish what is skillful and unskillful, and then progress through a traditional training sequence in which we learn (1) to replace unwanted thoughts, (2) to examine the risks of fueling habitual patterns, (3) to withdraw attention from toxic conditions, (4) to investigate causes, and (5) to exert dedicated resolve.

When applied in meditation, these strategies can strengthen our mental skills, lighten our psychological load, enhance our joy, increase stability of the mind, and lead us to life-changing insights. These ancient techniques are also relevant to everyday life. By understanding how the mind works, you can strengthen focused attention, clear away trivial distractions, organize your priorities, and reduce the destructive forces of craving, aversion, and delusion.

This book will help you unlock the incredible capacities of your mind to think clearly, reflect deeply, discern what is real, and pay attention to what is actually happening in your life. Real-life examples from meditation students who have worked with this training sequence demonstrate the relevance and value of each step. A range of pragmatic exercises will help you apply the lessons both on the cushion and in daily activities. By working with this training, you can develop skills to recognize the nature of your own mind and abandon unwholesome thought patterns.

These time-tested methods for overcoming distractions are needed now more than ever. The great twentieth-century Thai forest master, Ajahn Buddhadasa, was once asked how he would describe the state of the world today. He replied, "Lost in thought!" People spend an enormous portion of their lives dwelling in the stories they fabricate and exist largely disconnected from what is actually occurring in the present moment.

USEFUL BOTH IN MEDITATION AND DAILY ACTIVITIES

This is a book for meditators—both beginners who struggle to tame a restless mind and advanced meditators who strive to deepen their concentration and insight. The techniques presented here can be employed both on and off the meditation cushion and can support both spiritual and worldly success.

The techniques form a sequential training system. I recommend that you develop your skills systematically, chapter by chapter. Get comfortable applying one strategy before moving on to the next. Once you have gained some experience in working with this system for removing distracting thoughts, you can bypass the sequential order and apply whichever tool will be most effective in the given situation.

Whether you are an experienced meditator or a beginner trying to develop mindfulness, you probably know the pain of wrestling with an unruly, distracted mind. Before you can experience the extraordinary joy of a settled and concentrated mind, you must learn how to dispel distractions and overcome restlessness. Many kinds of disruptive thoughts can obstruct your concentration in meditation. In ordinary life these same distractions can lead to anxiety, insomnia, arrogance, procrastination, apathy, worry, and depression, while negatively impacting relationships, productivity, and your ease of mind.

As you learn to neutralize distraction and settle the mind, be assured that Buddhism does not reject rational or reflective mental activities—we need the ability to think clearly and function intelligently in this world. Critical thinking is an asset on a spiritual path. Too often, however, restlessness prevents us from effectively using our minds, and pervasive thoughts reinforce habits we might be happier without.

What Is Your Mind Doing?

Every day you use your mind in a wide variety of ways, both unproductive and productive. You might wake up feeling a bit worried about getting things done today, let your mind wander aimlessly during a morning shower, entertain fantasies through breakfast, apply the mind to solve problems at work, judge the performance of colleagues, contemplate philosophical questions, compose emails and letters, design playful games for your children, send a friend an encouraging message, accumulate knowledge through reading, and then relax into dreams at night.

You might notice that as you sit in meditation your mind may habitually wander away from your meditation practice and become caught up in worries or plans. Thoughts can take many entertaining forms. They can conjure up vivid stories and create a sense of self-orientation that organizes our perspectives on the world. Thoughts stimulate emotions, lead to actions, attribute meaning to events.

If you find that you are stuck in a mental rut, you can use your mind to investigate your thinking—in other words, become mindful of your mental activities.

Thoughts can be challenging objects for meditation because they occur in such rapid succession. The Buddha said, "I do not see even one other thing that changes so quickly as the mind. It is not easy to give a simile for how quickly the mind changes."[2]

Countless thoughts float through our minds every day. Impressions are woven into an intricate and seemingly inscrutable network of associations that shape how we view the world. While most thoughts zip past unnoticed, others reinforce perspectives that define our sense of self. If we think about a situation long enough, it is likely that—even without direct personal knowledge—we will develop beliefs based solely on the content of our repetitive thoughts. When meditators look closely at their minds, we are often aghast to discover how frequently thoughts reflect an obviously distorted perception of reality.

No Place to Stand

To see beyond habitual thoughts and to experience their emptiness, we must be familiar with the workings of the mind. Then, when the mind is not besieged by the compulsive fabrication of self-stories, we enjoy both calm serenity and profound freedom in life. The skillful removal of distracting thoughts not only will strengthen concentration but also is profoundly liberating. Freed from identification with thoughts, the mind may open to a quality of knowing beyond the realm of discursive, restless habits. As the fetter of restlessness weakens, profoundly freeing insights become available.

We learn to meet life intimately, experience feelings fully, and think clearly—all without taking experiences to be *I* and *mine*. There is an interesting term found in the Pāli discourses—*atammayatā*. It means "non-identification, non-fashioning, not constructing, not made of that." Atammayatā is the experience of not identifying with anything. It describes a rather advanced state of clarity in which we are not constructing self out of sensory experiences.

Not only has attachment to sensory experiences and personal identities ceased, but even attachment to subtle meditative attainments such as tranquility, equanimity, and insight knowledge has also ended. Delusions are not fabricated; personal opinions are not imposed upon perceptions. Atammayatā is a powerful state in which habitual defilements are at rest, and the trajectory of one's path is inclined toward liberation.

This experience of non-identification provides a clean lens through which we can more clearly comprehend the world of experience. From the perspective of atammayatā, whatever happens in the sensory field will be recognized as conditioned processes, without concocting a place for the self to stand.

Most meditators struggle just to let thoughts go, only to find themselves drawn right back into their stories. When we believe thoughts to be true, we may become entangled in the stories they tell and assume we *are* those distorted internal narratives.

The danger of allowing our thoughts to control us is illustrated in a line from the Pāli Canon in which a lazy meditator is warned, "You are eaten by your thoughts."[3] When consumed by our thoughts, we are unable to open to the liberating potential of the Buddhist path and the transformative insights into non-identification and emptiness.

While non-identification may sound like an appealing, fascinating, and far-off spiritual experience, it is achievable! To free ourselves from overwhelming thoughts, we can examine the conditioned patterns of mind that obscure the recognition that a thought is nothing more than a mental object being known by the mind.

TRAINING YOUR MIND

In this book you will learn to experience thoughts not as distracting impressions or incessant mental conversations that narrate your life story, but as discrete mental events (or states) that arise and pass away. At first it might seem impossible, especially for novice meditators, to distinguish a mental state from the content of a thought. As mindfulness gains momentum, however, the content of thoughts will naturally seem less enthralling.

You will notice the interplay between thoughts and physical sensations and watch as mental states and emotions affect perception. Both in your daily life and in your meditation practice, you will gradually recognize the patterns that influence your reactions. You will not only become mindful of your thoughts, but you will also discover how you relate to them, develop the skills to loosen the grip of unskillful thought patterns, and free your mind.

If you have a sincere interest in exploring your mind and follow along with the training sequence outlined in this book, you will learn a great deal about how your mind can either obstruct or support your spiritual path. The skills you learn will improve the clarity of daily decisions and ordinary activities, but the deeper purpose for training the mind is to see the emptiness of the thinking process and to cultivate the stability that supports liberating insight.

Neuroscientists have confirmed that the structure and function of the brain change in response to experience. It's encouraging to know that modern science agrees that our minds are pliable and can be transformed through training. Meditation not only calms the mind, but with diligent practice it develops mental flexibility, malleability, and clarity. As the Buddha described, one's mind "becomes malleable, wieldy, and luminous, pliant and properly concentrated for the destruction of the taints."[4]

⁓⁓ *Join an Online Course to Support Your Practice*

Readers may wish to supplement this book with Shaila Catherine's online course, Beyond Distraction: Practical Strategies to Free the Mind.

For information about her online Dhamma classroom, visit:

Bodhi Courses
www.bodhicourses.org

By gradually freeing your mind from deluded thinking patterns and the fetter of restlessness, you may experience the deep rest of tranquil states and open the door to the liberating insight of emptiness that is at the heart of the Buddhist path of awakening.

THE INSPIRATION FOR THIS BOOK

This book is inspired by two ancient teachings found in the *Middle Length Discourses of the Buddha*: the Dvedhāvitakka Sutta: Two Kinds of Thought, and the Vitakkasaṇṭhāna Sutta: The Removal of Distracting Thoughts.[5] These teachings present a sequence of practical strategies for removing obstructive mental patterns that can be applied in both meditation and daily life situations.

The Buddha tells us that before his enlightenment, he sometimes found his mind preoccupied by thoughts connected with sensual desire, ill will, and harming. He was not, however, daunted by distracting thoughts. He figured out how to deal with thoughts skillfully and developed a step-by-step approach to calm the restless mind. The Buddha's pragmatic instructions inform this little book. They have guided generations of meditators and have the potential to radically transform how you use your own mind.

You do not need to live enslaved by habitual thought patterns. I encourage you to take up the challenge and free yourself from distracting thoughts. Work with the many exercises offered in this book. Learn about your own mind and develop the capacity to think what you want to think. In the moment you recognize that a thought is just a thought, you will find yourself on the path to a life of remarkable freedom.

SUMMARY OF MAIN POINTS

The mind can be a potent tool, used to guide extraordinary achievements, inspire good works, and incline you toward spiritual realization. But it can also produce thoughts that lead to suffering. For many people, thoughts run rampant and seem to oppress or control their lives. You can learn to overcome habitual modes of thinking to support worldly success, deeper concentration, and insights into emptiness that characterize a liberating spiritual path.

CHAPTER 1

KNOWING YOUR OWN MIND

Many Kinds of Thoughts

"Thoughts are understood as they arise, understood as they remain present, understood as they pass away."
—Connected Discourses of the Buddha[6]

EACH OF US has developed our own personal array of mental habits that affect the choices we make and the way we experience, interpret, and respond in life. Whenever we sit down to meditate, these habits continue to operate, and we can observe them. What is the mind doing? What do we want our minds to be doing?

Some people chat with themselves, as a child would with an invisible friend. Others might narrate past events, spinning the story toward their personal advantage. One might hear fragments of a tune floating through his or her mind or ponder design options for a potential kitchen remodel. A recently retired person might lie awake at night rehearsing project proposals and imagining how former colleagues would respond. Someone who purchases a weekly lottery ticket might conjure up detailed plans for spending the ten-million-dollar jackpot. Because mental chatter is such a common habit, meditation students often long for thought-free bliss and wonder, "Will my mind ever settle? Will I ever know the peace and joy of a quiet mind?"

The wandering mind seems ubiquitous. Using fMRI scans, researchers discovered brain activity in subjects who were not engaged in mental tasks but were resting quietly.

The group of brain regions that shows lower-level activity when we engage in an activity that requires attention and a higher-level activity when we are awake but resting is now known as the "default mode network." The default mode network has been found to be particularly active when the mind is wandering, craving, or engaging in self-referential thinking. Conversely, the default mode network has been found to be consistently deactivated during activities that require focused attention, mindful awareness, and engagement in present tasks.

Researchers continue to explore what happens in the brain when we get caught up in our experiences and find ourselves lost in thought.[7]

Several studies found that the default mode network of adept meditators is remarkably quieter than that of novice meditators or the general population. It may be true that minds tend to wander, and that thinking is a natural activity of the mind. However, mindfulness and meditation practices can significantly quiet the mind.[8]

In the training sequence presented in this book, we begin by working with overt, repetitive thoughts that tend to be charged with emotion or to develop into full-fledged stories. These techniques are intended to be applied as needed to dispel distractions that obstruct the development of concentration and clear seeing. As mindfulness becomes more refined, you may sometimes become aware of a subtle stream of deluded impressions that seem to arise without a clear cause and then disappear before crystallizing into coherent ideas. This subtle level of mental activity will also gradually subside as tranquility develops.

In daily life, an agitated mind can be burdensome. It feels even worse if the scenarios you rehearse, the worries you entertain, the opinions you promote, and the memories you cherish are tinged with self-judgment, are biased, or are outright false. Mental chatter not only wastes time and energy but tends to follow circular patterns of thought that solidify your distorted perspective.

Memories can easily be distorted to fit into your current narrative. For example, if you are influenced to think negatively about a person, you tend to have primarily negative memories and to predict similar, unhappy experiences in the future. Relationships are reinforced through selective memories. Minor past events might be exaggerated to unconsciously prove that the judgments are accurate, that *I am right*. After all, you probably rarely lose an argument that takes place only in your head.

According to Buddhist teachings, perception is inherently limited, conditioned by physical and mental processes. Variations in visual, olfactory, and auditory acuity among people shape their individual perceptions. In the same way, emotions, biases, desires, preferences, defilements, beliefs, fears, memories, and previous experiences affect perception. In addition, what one assumes about oneself as the perceiving subject inevitably distorts the perception of the object.

THOUGHTS ARE MENTAL EVENTS

A meditative exploration of mind depends upon clearly distinguishing between the *content* of your thoughts and the *process* of thinking.

If you give too much emphasis to the content of a thought, you might not realize that thoughts are the objects of discrete mental events. A narrative might appear to have a sense of coherence and continuity, but by looking closely you will see that the cognitive events that form the story arise and pass away quite rapidly. A memory or fantasy might seem so real that you experience pleasure, pain, emotion, and sensation as the story unfolds in your mind. Take care not to believe the content and become immersed in the narratives, or delusion will run the show.

To investigate your thoughts in meditation you need only establish a cursory awareness of the narrative content—just enough to determine whether pursuing this train of thought is moving you toward trouble or ease, happiness or suffering, bondage or release. Look closely at a thought but refrain from brooding on its content or becoming enchanted by its narrative. What is actually happening right now? Your answer might be simple, perhaps just "thinking is happening."

Whatever patterns your mind tends to adopt, notice that the thought content is not the objective reality. The story line is not happening in the outside objective world; rather, a process of thinking is occurring.

When you recognize the event called *thinking*, you have become mindful of the activity that you are currently engaged in. This honest and clear engagement with present experience paves the way for skillfully developing your mind. After recognizing that thinking is occurring, you can consider whether this use of your mind is nourishing your deepest goals or obstructing them.

Beginning meditators usually first learn basic skills that protect the mind from being sucked into the realm of thoughts. For example, one might direct attention away from thinking and focus attention on present sensations of the body while sitting and breathing. Additional meditative skills work directly with thoughts and the mental states that accompany them.

When you can turn your attention toward a thought without being seduced by the story line, you will be able to explore your tendencies, patterns, and the intentions that propel speech and action.

MANY KINDS OF THOUGHTS

As you notice the thoughts that float through your mind, you may find distinct patterns that you easily recognize to be harmful. Other patterns that run through your mind each day may not seem overtly cruel, greedy, or hateful. It might not be obvious whether they cause problems, yet you may sense that they do not support your spiritual life. The discussion in this and subsequent chapters will explore a wide range of patterns that may obstruct your concentration, including patterns that do not appear to be particularly evil.

For example, patterns of rehearsing, worrying, planning, judging, analyzing, remembering, replaying, anticipating, expecting, designing, strategizing, ruminating, and pondering are not as acutely destructive as hateful thoughts of plotting revenge. At times we need to plan, rehearse, remember, analyze, and design. The fully awakened *arahant* disciples of the Buddha engaged in some of these activities when they remembered, pondered, rehearsed, recited, and analyzed the teachings that they had learned. Although these ways of thinking are not inherently unwholesome, for some of us they can become compulsive habits that distort perception, divert energy away from concentration and insight, reinforce a deluded self-position, and prevent us from being fully present with life as it is unfolding right now.

Please consider the thoughts that have crossed your mind today. What kinds of thoughts caught your attention and occupied your mental energy? Was there one primary obsession or a flurry of trivial thoughts? Did the character you call *myself* have a leading role or did it narrate the story to an imagined audience? What was the outcome of your mental activity? Anticipating future events, ruminating over past mistakes, obsessively solving everyone else's problems, and entertaining yourself with your own life stories might appear to be innocuous mental activities, but these habits place an enormous

Recognizing Restlessness in Daily Activities

Observe the various kinds of thoughts in your mind while performing your daily activities. Notice clues to the state of your mind and keep a watch out for signs of restlessness while engaged in social encounters and ordinary activities. For example, notice if you become restless and distracted in daily activities. Observe:

- ▸ The quality of your sleep and how long it takes before you fall asleep
- ▸ Cravings for food, drink, or shopping, or an urge to check your communication devices for messages or emails
- ▸ Nervous tics or restless movements
- ▸ Excessive gregariousness or silent withdrawal
- ▸ Degrees of frowning, smiling, and facial tension
- ▸ Willingness or unwillingness to make eye contact

You might notice your mood, your behavior, the attitudes or responses of other people toward you, your analytical reflections, and the thoughts that arise after an event. Do you feel more selfish or more compassionate in the wake of restless thoughts? Learn to notice the signals that help you determine whether your engagement is wholesome or unwholesome and whether it is likely to be beneficial or harmful in that particular situation.

burden on the mind. Day in and day out, they reinforce distorted and deluded perceptions of yourself. In meditation they hinder deep concentration and insight.

Observe Thoughts

When you are involved in thinking, pause and notice thoughts as just thoughts. They are momentary, discrete mental events; they are not necessarily telling a true story.

Notice what kind of thoughts arise most frequently in your mind. How would you categorize your most common thought patterns? For example, do they involve mental activities such as planning, controlling, worrying, judging, expecting, comparing, analyzing, ruminating, or craving? Are your habits feeding boredom or curiosity, arrogance or humility, envy or appreciation, irritation or patience? Is your mind stuck in low-grade, chronic distraction and trivial meandering?

Watch your mind and notice the underlying themes that play out in the scenarios you think about. Observe the habitual thoughts that float through your meditation. Observe the thoughts that occur as you shower and brush your teeth. Observe the thoughts in the background of consciousness while you commute to and from work or go to and from the grocery store. Observe the thoughts that come to bed with you and the first thoughts that appear as you are waking up. Throughout the day, observe your thoughts to notice the mental patterns that influence your perceptions.

Gradually unpack the myriad ways habitual thoughts feed on delusion, distort perception, perpetuate restlessness, and obstruct the clarity of your wisdom. At times you might protest, "But these thoughts are entertaining, creative, interesting, and soothing!" Indeed, sometimes thoughts are delightful and lead to valuable insights. Learn to notice and name the many kinds of thoughts that arise in a day and see what they produce. Notice whether these activities of thought support your present activity or distract your attention from what you are doing now. Some thoughts might be useful on the job but could be detrimental at the family breakfast table or during a meditation session.

Here are a few common thought patterns you might notice.

Daydreaming

Daydreaming can make people oblivious to what is happening in the world around them. As you become entranced by the tale, it might feel like you are the producer, director, scriptwriter, and costume designer for a play. You might be the heroic character, the victim, the predator, the innocent bystander, or the narrator.

Although you might believe these thoughts are creative and fresh and even imagine that you are in control of the narrative, they are just conditioned thoughts. When you are lost in a fantasy, you are not mindful of what is real. Such imaginary scenarios often solidify a capricious fiction—the story of self. Variations of the self-story lie behind most common thoughts. Subsequent chapters of this book will explore this type of self-fabrication in greater detail.

Romantic Fantasies

Pleasure fantasies can seduce the mind. Stimulated perhaps by little more than a brief glimpse of an attractive stranger at the bus stop, a mind inclined to romantic fantasy might become lost in thoughts of an imaginary relationship. No matter how detailed the fantasies might be, they are not real—yet the investment of time and emotion can make them seem so! Dwelling in pleasure fantasies may attribute undue importance to unlikely scenarios and feed dissatisfaction with the way things really are. Further, every moment you opt to indulge this form of craving, you are choosing to disconnect rather than become mindful and aware of what is actually present now.

Judging, Ranking, Comparing

We can all agree that some people have skills that others do not. For example, some people have greater physical strength or athletic agility. Others have an impressive intellect, a keen eye for detail, or a powerful memory. For some people meditation is easy and observing the mind is fun, while for others a Herculean effort is needed just to muster up the discipline to meditate.

Comparing and judging require both an evaluator and some criteria for evaluation. As evaluators, we can delude ourselves that our criteria are objective and our ability to assess is accurate, but our comparisons are inherently biased.

Although we cannot accurately assess our personal significance or define ourselves through comparison, many of our thoughts attempt to do so. Such thought patterns repeat and embellish previous assumptions, reinforcing the personal and social identity from which they arose.

Ask yourself, do you ever rank yourself against others in a group? Do you compare your appearance, abilities, or status with those of your peers? Do you assess your degree of belonging or social power by comparing it to that of colleagues? Do you position yourself as better, worse, or equal to neighbors, relatives, or public figures?

In many practical situations, however, comparing is useful. Mindfulness practice will not inhibit your ability to compare products in order to purchase the one most suitable for your needs. Nor will meditation limit your ability to choose teachers, friends, and mentors wisely. By watching the comparing mind, you will notice when comparing is helpful and when it perpetuates attachment to a fabricated self-image.

Some comparisons might seem to improve self-esteem. "I got a promotion faster than she did. My car is newer than his. The product I bought is better than this other product. My team did better than yours." However, such comparisons can also nurture conceit and arrogance. Negative comparisons can magnify self-critical tendencies with thoughts such as "I'm uglier, sicker, poorer, dumber." Comparing is at best relative, based on temporary conditions, and not a reliable strategy for nourishing self-respect.

Comparing arises not only between individuals but also between groups. This can cultivate the notion that one is entitled to greater privilege simply because one is born as a male or female; has light or dark skin; is the heir of a family lineage or member of a dominant or minority group; belongs to a certain organization, culture, or nation; or aligns with a particular religious or political philosophy.

From the limited perspective of our personal circumstances, comparisons seem to have meaning, but the results of comparisons differ depending on the point of view from which they are made. Is a curry mild or spicy? The answer will depend on your flavor preferences. Is a toothpick short or long? It might depend on whether a human or an ant is trying to carry it. Is a month a long time or a short time? It might be a long time to bake a pizza or a short time to master the flute. All comparisons depend on the viewpoint and bias through which they are perceived, and therefore none of them can be said to be objectively true.

In many modern societies competition is encouraged at school, at work, and even in leisure activities. In such environments, the habit of judging and comparing can become deeply ingrained. It might be common for people to compare themselves against impossible ideals or turn ordinary activities into intense competitions.

If excessive criticism or unrelenting competitiveness is souring your relationships, or harsh self-judgments are thwarting your ability to grow, notice the ways that a habitually judging mind might be causing suffering. Consider: do you really have the knowledge, expertise, and qualifications to fairly and wisely judge this situation?

The Buddha discussed the pattern of passing judgment on others and considered who would be capable of accurately assessing the attainments and results of another's spiritual practice. He cautioned, "Do not pass judgment on people. Those who pass judgment on people harm themselves. I alone, or one like me, may pass judgment on people."[9] To cultivate wise discernment without becoming chronically judgmental, notice when your mind is engaged in comparing, and consider, "Do I really have the knowledge, experience, and expertise to wisely pass judgement here?"

Planning

A healthy, active, and successful life will undoubtedly involve personal organization, financial planning, and perhaps strategic business plans. Most activities require some degree of preparation. Perhaps you must decide what you will cook for dinner in a way that utilizes the vegetables that are ripening in your garden. You might plan for emergencies by having supplies on hand. You might plan the steps you will take to complete a building project or home repair. Before leaving your home to do errands, you might find it useful to write out a grocery list and take a moment to plan your route.

The spiritual life is not devoid of plans. You might intentionally structure your meditation practice to use a sequence of steps to settle your mind and strengthen mindfulness. You might use systematic methods to broaden your meditative skills or cultivate wholesome qualities. You might follow a variety of gradual step-by-step methods that are taught in Buddhist traditions. Directing attention through predetermined sequences might technically be included in this category of planning, but they are not hindrances to meditation. For the most part, however, planning worldly events during meditation and attachment to planned outcomes are common distractions.

Whether during meditation or in daily life, if your mind obsessively rehearses conversations that may never happen, mentally packs for a holiday trip you hope to take next year, or envisions how you will experience the rest of your life, your planning activities have probably slid beyond the range of usefulness.

ᨳ *Watching Thoughts*

Notice the kinds of thoughts that arise during your daily activities. Choose one or two activities, such as showering, washing the dishes, or eating breakfast. During those activities, diligently notice your own thoughts, distinguishing between the helpful thoughts and those that are hurtful. In a notebook or on a sheet of paper, jot down a few of the kinds of thoughts you noticed.

Identify specific types of thought such as worry, planning, blaming, judging, rehearsing, controlling, comparing, analyzing.

Do these modes of thinking tend to arise when you are meditating? Going to bed? Eating? Driving? Getting dressed in the morning? Walking the dog? Mopping the floor? Making dinner for your family? Helping your kids with their homework? Waiting for an appointment? Between projects?

You might make one list of wholesome thoughts and another list of unwholesome thoughts. Notice whether those thoughts persist or repeat or whether your tendencies change over the course of this week. Does simply recognizing your thought patterns have an effect on the tendency to think one way or another way?

A great deal of planning is motivated by the delusion that one can control the future. No matter how well you have rehearsed how you will appear when you walk into the office, what you will say to your spouse at dinner, or how you will feel when your doctor explains the biopsy results, you cannot fully control dynamics that involve other people. Life is not a screenplay where the cast reads from carefully edited scripts.

It can be useful to prepare for difficult communications by reflecting on your intentions and options, but obsessive thinking is not preparation. Overthinking is likely a manifestation of restlessness and worry. Notice whether you catch your mind in a whirl of imagined potential responses. "If she does this, I will say that. If this happens, then I will do that." Repeated *if-then* scenarios magnify the delusion of control and are common indicators that planning has gone too far.

Mindfulness meditation cultivates the ability to be present to what actually is occurring, right here and now. When you are mindful, you will be more confident that you can meet each situation with interest and clarity, without manipulating events to conform to preconceived plans. You will be equipped to respond to what is really occurring, not to your fantasies, worries, and fears.

If you notice that planning scenarios are distracting you from present-moment experience in meditation, set a limit to the planning. First, notice what you are planning and name it. Look for happily-ever-after fairytales, packing fantasies, shopping lists, looking-smart strategies, getting-the-last-word plans, making-an-impression ideas. Then set a limit to the proliferation. For example, allow three versions of the plan, but then firmly put a stop to it. Or exert sufficient determination to quell those thoughts just for the duration of your sitting meditation. By suspending your obsession with planning for a modest period of time, you may find that later you are able to consider your plans with a fresh, creative, clear perspective.

Instructing

Do you hear an inner voice telling yourself what to do? An internal voice of guidance might be helpful in small doses—sometimes you might give yourself excellent advice! The pattern of instructing, however, can become a problem when it exceeds moderation, is infused with blame, or is distorted by feelings of insecurity. If you carry your instructing tendency into your relationships, you might appear to be a know-it-all. Your good advice might be marred by arrogance and the attempt to control.

During meditation, this pattern of instructing might shift your focus from mindfulness of present experience to composing a lesson about meditating. Good meditative advice is usually very simple, like the reminder to be interested in what is happening right now. Any instruction that you provide to yourself should enhance your mindfulness, not interrupt your mindfulness, and not distort your experience by comparing it to spiritual concepts.

Evaluating Your Practice

When you meditate, you are actively cultivating your mind. You do not, however, need to narrate a blow-by-blow commentary as your meditative experience unfolds, boast to your friends about how mindful you have become, meditate in public to show off your upright sitting posture, track your progress according to traditional levels of spiritual attainments, anticipate the feeling you might have during your next meditation session, crave the joy or luminosity that might occur in meditation, competitively log your sitting time on meditation apps, or grasp onto signs of spiritual success.

Awakening experiences do happen, but meditators who are attached to spiritual maps and overly concerned with attainments might actually impair their own progress by imagining having an extraordinary experience before the actual experience genuinely occurs or fully matures.

Ruminating

The mind can sometimes become enmeshed in rehashing past mistakes. Feeding on guilt or harsh self-judgments, rumination can prevent you from learning from your errors and moving forward in life. A ruminating mind might replay past hurts with such intensity that reactions of fear, anger, and pain are triggered. Past traumas can feel terrifyingly real, as though one is reliving painful events in the present moment. When revisiting the past, the defensive mind might alter the story or weave alternative outcomes into the narrative and thereby distort the picture of what actually occurred.

If you find yourself in a pattern of ruminations, ask yourself what is feeding them. What is their purpose? Although it is useful to reflect and learn from our past actions, excessive rumination is a trap. It leads to a sense of disconnection with the present, and it does not support the kind of wise reflection that promotes insight.

Problem-Solving

Mulling over problems in search of solutions is another form of obsessive thinking. This inclination to identify issues and prescribe advice shares some characteristics with planning, ruminating, worrying, and analyzing. For many people, problem-solving is fun. Inventions, game strategies, engineering puzzles, and many creative pursuits utilize the remarkable capacity of the mind to solve problems. It can be rewarding to instigate a plan, watch how the strategy plays out, adjust the game plan as conditions change, and follow a line of thinking until the goal is achieved.

Although the problem-solving mind can lead to accomplishments, if misdirected it can create conflicts. Not everyone will welcome your interference in their life situations. Excessive strategizing can also exhaust the mind, inhibit your capacity to be present with current conditions, and foster the arrogant illusion that you are in control and that you know best. Problem-solving becomes an obstacle when this pattern of mind arises in inappropriate contexts, manifests along with restlessness, and adorns the ego.

Problem-solving skills can also produce creative and effective solutions when employed in appropriate contexts. For example, during meditation you might notice that angry thoughts are arising, and by recognizing this as an obstacle to your peace of mind, you are inspired to seek an antidote or apply strategies to overcome the obstacle. The many strategies presented in this book could be seen as solutions to the problems that are produced by unskillful mental habits.

Summary of Main Points

Thoughts are discrete mental events. Just as you may be mindful of sounds or sensations, you can also become mindful of thoughts as they arise and pass away.

You do not need to be carried away by thoughts; you don't have to follow them or embellish their narratives. The content of thought does not exist as an objective reality in the world.

Learn to notice and name the many kinds of thoughts that arise in a day: daydreaming, fantasizing, judging or comparing, planning, instructing, ruminating, strategizing. Some thoughts that appear innocuous or beneficial in worldly situations do not support calmness, concentration, and wisdom in your spiritual practice. Avoid letting the ways you think reinforce attachment to deluded assumptions about self.

❧ *Kinds of Thinking during Meditation*

Devote most of your meditation session to your usual mindfulness practice, but when thoughts pull you away from your meditation object or recurring stories entangle your mind, investigate this pattern with the following approaches.

Notice that thinking is happening as a changing mental event that may take the form of mental words, narratives, or images. Distinguish between the *process* of thinking and the *content* of the thought. To help identify the thinking process, you might add a mental label such as *thinking* to intensify the recognition that thinking is occurring.

What kind of thought process is happening? If the type of thought is clear to you, apply a specific label rather than the general term *thinking*—you might note it as *comparing*, *fantasizing*, *planning*, *worrying*, or *reminiscing*. If the type of thought is not immediately clear, simply note it as *thinking*.

Is it a wholesome or unwholesome thought? Notice the cues that help you determine whether the thought is beneficial or likely to lead to harm. For example, cues might come in the form of:

- ▸ bodily sensations, tension, comfort, or pain
- ▸ changes in temperature or blood pressure
- ▸ mental agitation or calm
- ▸ shifts in body posture

Learn to notice the signals that help you determine whether this is a wholesome or unwholesome thought, and whether it is beneficial or harmful.

CHAPTER 2

THOUGHTS THAT HELP AND THOUGHTS THAT HURT

What Intentions Do You Nurture?

Whatever one frequently thinks and ponders upon,
that will become the inclination of the mind.
—MIDDLE LENGTH DISCOURSES OF THE BUDDHA[10]

BEFORE HIS ENLIGHTENMENT and while he was still striving for the goal of awakening, the Buddha-to-be decided to divide his thoughts into two classes. He set on one side thoughts that were unwholesome (*akusala*). Connected with sensual desire, ill will, and cruelty, these thoughts produce suffering. On the other side, he set wholesome thoughts (*kusala*). Connected with renunciation, non–ill will, and noncruelty, these thoughts generate happiness.[11] These six classifications of thoughts (three wholesome and three unwholesome) condition actions of body, speech, and mind.

Some readers may prefer alternative translations for the terms *kusala* and *akusala*: profitable and unprofitable, skillful and unskillful, beneficial and harmful, good and bad. The three wholesome and three unwholesome thoughts are also called *three right intentions* and *three wrong intentions*. Whichever terms you prefer, the growth of wisdom depends upon distinguishing between what supports the path of awakening and what perpetuates suffering. As practice develops, you may discover that by abandoning an unskillful thought you create the space for a better alternative to flourish.

People might assume that allowing the mind to wander and seeking sensual pleasures are innocuous, entertaining, relaxing pursuits. Replaying scenes from the movie you watched last week, mentally narrating your actions as you perform a complicated task, or allowing your mind to follow random associations may not seem terribly harmful, but neuroscientists have confirmed that the wandering mind is generally associated with unhappy states.[12]

Importantly, in the early discourses of the Buddha we find many descriptions of meditators who have dispelled distraction and are living with few comforts but experience joy, bliss, and the profound pleasures of concentrated states. One king described the community of monastics as "smiling and cheerful, sincerely joyful, plainly delighting, their faculties fresh, living at ease, unruffled . . ."[13]

When Buddhist teachings categorize sensual desire as a defilement, they are not opposing joy, happiness, or the recognition of pleasant sensory events.

Pleasant sense-based experiences such as sights, sounds, and sensations are also welcome and considered normal aspects of life. One of the great disciples of the Buddha, Venerable Mahākaccāna, delivered a discourse on the diversity of feelings and stated, "In dependence on a contact to be experienced as pleasant there arises a pleasant feeling." This straightforward recognition of pleasures does not resist or deny pleasant feelings. He then encourages meditators to experience pleasure knowing that it is pleasant, with the recognition "such it is."[14]

Pleasant experiences are not intrinsically obstructive to the spiritual path. But the *pursuit of* sensual pleasures, *desire for* sensual pleasures, and *obsessive thoughts about* sensual pleasures function as hindrances to concentration and distractions on the path of awakening.

When you notice that you are craving sensual pleasures—such as a favorite food or the attention of a friend—investigate that mental state. You will probably find that the desire for sensual pleasure is accompanied by conditions that are obviously unwholesome—lack of mindfulness or equanimity, obsessive thinking, deluded fantasies, absence of attention to the impermanence of feeling, tendency toward possessiveness, craving for what is not present, discontent with what is present, restlessness, and identification with personal desire.

A succession of thoughts that justify the desire might embolden it, and those justifications might become a recurring distraction even after the pleasant event has passed. Strong sensual desire may weaken your capacity for ethical restraint, making you more willing to cause harm to others as you pursue the pleasure. When you indulge memories of past sensual experiences, revel in present sensual pleasures, attempt to sustain current pleasant feelings, and scheme to increase future delights, progress toward tranquility and insight will be blocked.

Sensual desires are not limited to sexual desire. In this book, I use the terms and phrases *desire for sensual pleasure*, *sensual lust*, and *sensual desire* to imply the tangled mental states of greed, distraction, obsession, and discontent that occur in conjunction with craving. The defilements that we abandon occur in this unhealthy mental condition.

In contrast, you may enjoy a delicious mouthful of garlic mashed potato and fully experience the pleasant buttery texture and perfectly salted flavor without remorse. You may soak in a hot spring, happy that the warm waters relax your muscles and relieve your aching back. You may wander through a museum impressed by great works of art, appreciate the loving touch of your partner, and feel comforted by the soft purr of your cat as she curls up on your lap. You can enjoy the many pleasant experiences of life while still being committed to the path of liberation, but don't let the pursuit of pleasures thwart the deepening of your concentration or the clarity of insight. Don't let pleasant experiences reinforce craving, restlessness, and delusion in your mind.

While Buddhist teachings highlight the pitfalls of craving temporary sensual pleasures, the teachings encourage people to actively cultivate the more trustworthy happiness that comes with spiritual development. Happiness associated with virtue, meditation, and wisdom is prized. As the Buddha explicitly stated, "there is another kind of happiness more excellent and sublime" than sensual pleasure.[15]

By working with your own mind, you will discover how a wholesome mind is a profoundly happy mind. When intentions are beneficial, our minds tend to be balanced, settled, mindful, and harmonious. In contrast, when our intentions are unwholesome, our minds tend to be agitated, our thoughts are affected by a sense of deficiency or insecurity, and we tend to act in selfish or greedy ways.

Thoughts of Sensual Desire versus Thoughts of Renunciation

Compare the quality of your mind when you are driven by a longing for sensual desire with its quality when you feel inspired to let go. You will probably find that thoughts of sensual desire are connected with anxiety, frustration, compulsion, and a sense of agitation. When the mind wants something, it is discontent. In contrast, the intention to let go and renounce attachments nourishes contentment, gratitude, generosity, and ease.

When you intentionally nourish wholesome qualities and experience the rewards of wholesome states, attachment to unwholesome sensual pursuits will weaken, and the habit of craving will lose its grip on your mind.

Encouraged by the Reward

To highlight the experiential difference between whole-some and unwholesome intentions, recall something good, perhaps something that you feel gratitude or appreciation for, such as good friendship, favorable conditions, a for-tunate opportunity, or having helped someone. Notice whether you feel joy, happiness, or pleasure when you think of something you appreciate and are grateful for.

You can strengthen your inclination toward whole-some thoughts by becoming more aware of the rewards of wholesome pleasures. Let the nonsensuous feeling of joy suffuse your mind for several moments. Then intentionally enhance thoughts of contentment for that beneficial con-dition. Every day, notice occasions that produce a skillful nonsensuous joy, and let the pleasant feelings associated with wholesome thoughts pervade your mind.

If you are not convinced that wholesome nonsensuous pleasures are rewarding, then as an experiment, bring to mind something that you believe is lacking in your life. Observe your feelings and mental states. Did you notice a shift in your mental state? Did craving, wanting, fear, or disappointment arise?

How would you describe the difference between your experience of contentment vs. that of craving?

Thoughts of Ill Will versus Thoughts of Kindness

Notice how you feel when ill will festers in your mind and deter-mines your actions. A mind driven by ill will is usually irritable, angry, judgmental, fearful, and insecure. On the other hand, a mind imbued with loving-kindness is often happy, serene, loving, and trustworthy.

Thoughts of Harming versus Thoughts of Compassion

Consider what happens when thoughts of harming proliferate. They can magnify feelings of resentment, distrust, jealous insecurities, obsession with betrayals, and the fear of being inadequate. But, when one relates to others with compassion, the mind is upbeat, the ability to trust others grows, and strong friendships are built.

WHICH THOUGHTS WILL YOU NURTURE?

Once you recognize that you don't need to buy into the content of your thoughts, you can step back to observe thought for what it is. This observational stance creates the possibility to choose what kind of thoughts you will entertain. This attitude can be seen in the Buddha's description of his experiences prior to his awakening:

> As I abided thus, diligent, ardent, and resolute, a thought of sensual desire arose in me. I understood thus: "This thought of sensual desire has arisen in me. This leads to my own affliction, to others' affliction, and to the affliction of both; it obstructs wisdom, causes difficulties, and leads away from Nibbāna." When I considered: "This leads to my own affliction," it subsided in me; when I considered: "This leads to others' affliction," it subsided in me; when I considered: "This leads to the affliction of both," it subsided in me; when I considered: "This obstructs wisdom, causes difficulties, and leads away from Nibbāna," it subsided in me. Whenever a thought of sensual desire arose in me, I abandoned it, removed it, did away with it.[16]

Make Two Piles

Settle into meditation by anchoring mindfulness with an awareness of the breath or body. When the mind wanders into thoughts, welcome this opportunity for investigation.

1. Recognize that this is a thought. Label it as *thinking*.
2. Ask yourself, is it a helpful or harmful thought? Notice how you determine whether it is wholesome or unwholesome. What physical or emotional cues told you that this was likely to be helpful or hurtful?
3. Imagine a game where you toss the wholesome thoughts to the left and the unwholesome ones to the right. Make two piles. Alternative games would be to imagine tossing frisbees or balls in different directions. Some meditation students like to add an imaginary third pile for thoughts that are useful in work and daily activities but not supportive of meditative development.
4. Between each toss, bring the mind back to the body breathing.
5. When you notice that another thought has arisen, move through the sequence again.

Use this game to relate to the thoughts as simply fabricated mental objects, not indications of who you are.

INTENTIONS

Intentions—thoughts that lead to actions—have an enormous impact on our lives, whether we are conscious of the quality of our thoughts or not. Split second by split second, in every moment of our day, intentions arise, affect the choices we make, shape our actions, and condition our experience of life.

It is the quality of the *intention* behind an action that defines the act of body, speech, or mind as wholesome or unwholesome. The same action might be beneficial or harmful depending upon the intention. For example, plunging a knife into someone's body is surely unwholesome when the intention is to kill the person. A surgeon, however, might make skillful incisions while trying to save that person's life.

As a meditator, if you value the possibility of awakening, you willingly examine not only the intentions you set for your meditation practice but also the wide array of intentions that underlie your physical, verbal, and mental actions. You can determine whether your actions are fed by lust, greed, hate, anger, delusion, or conceit, and you can resolve to respond in ways that nourish only beneficial intentions and actions.

As presented in the discourse on Two Kinds of Thought, the Buddha's teachings highlight the three right and three wrong intentions. In subsequent chapters, the teachings in the discourse on the Removal of Distracting Thoughts focus on the influence of three root poisons that affect thoughts—greed, anger, and delusion.

Exploring the intentions that affect your actions and dispelling the root poisons that condition emotional patterns that influence your mental activity create space for the mind to become clear, calm, and happy. Nourishing wisdom, loving-kindness, and contentment trains your mind toward wholesome rather than distracting conditions.

Through diligent practice, you can gradually free your mind from the corrupting forces of greed, hate, and delusion.

 Formulating Your Intentions

Our intentions have a significant impact on our actions. Please give some thought to why you are practicing meditation. What is your aim, your goal, your inspiration and aspiration? Articulate those intentions with a simple sentence or two. Write them down.

Reflect on your purpose and goals at the beginning of each meditation session, in the morning when you wake up, and before important actions. Use whatever phrasing suits you and enhances your genuine and deep motivations. Here are some examples:

- ▸ May my actions today contribute to peace and happiness in this world.
- ▸ May my meditation practice be a contributing cause for the realization of Nibbāna.
- ▸ May I act in ways that increase the welfare and happiness of those around me.
- ▸ Let equanimity and renunciation support this decision.
- ▸ I will focus my attention to clearly see how I-making occurs.
- ▸ May delusion be dispelled.

WE GET GOOD AT WHAT WE PRACTICE

Repeated intentions form the recurring traits that continue to influence our future actions. Your current thoughts arose due to conditions. Your reaction to current thoughts reinforces those tendencies and facilitates the occurrence of similar reactions in the future. Repeated actions develop into habits that manifest as dispositional traits. Those traits and dispositional tendencies condition further actions. In this way, the cycle rolls on.

The Buddha's teachings highlight the influence that repeated thoughts can have on our minds:

> Whatever one frequently thinks and ponders upon, that will become the inclination of one's mind. If one frequently thinks and ponders upon thoughts of sensual desire, one has abandoned the thoughts of renunciation to cultivate the thoughts of sensual desire, and then one's mind inclines to thoughts of sensual desire. If one frequently thinks and ponders upon thoughts of ill will . . . upon thoughts of cruelty, one has abandoned the thoughts of non-cruelty to cultivate the thoughts of ill will and cruelty, and then one's mind inclines to thoughts of cruelty.[17]

Repetition strengthens patterns—we get good at the things we practice. When we frequently repeat a pattern, we strengthen those neural pathways, and those thoughts or reactions arise more easily in the future. For example, if we indulge in angry judgmental tirades, anger will increasingly arise quickly and require progressively weaker triggers. If we expect to always get what we want, pleasure-seeking behaviors will occur without restraint.

Habits are like channels in the mind—energies, thoughts, and actions tend to flow in the direction of the groove that has already formed. So, notice: How are you participating in the conditioning of your mind? What patterns are you practicing? What kind of habit grooves are you carving?

In the discourse on Two Kinds of Thought, the Buddha uses the simile of a cowherd, who in the autumn when the crops are thick must vigorously check and curb his cows by poking them to keep them out of the crops. If he allowed the cows to graze on the crops, he could be fined or punished. When the danger of temptation is nearby, do you notice habitual patterns and curb unskillful tendencies? Do you protect yourself from future harm by training your mind to choose wiser actions?

 ### *Mindful of Mind from Morning to Night*

Insert several thirty-second reflections into your daily schedule to examine the quality of your mind. Look at your mind with the intention of noticing:

- ► What thoughts are present? Name the kind of thought.
- ► Is your present mental state beneficial or detrimental?
- ► Is it causing trouble for yourself or others?
- ► Does it support or obstruct your deeper values and goals?

Gradually build a continuity of mindful interest in the state of your mind as it changes throughout the day. Notice how the simple effort to observe the mind with wisdom can diminish unwholesome patterns and strengthen wholesome states.

We all have different tendencies and are vulnerable to our own unique combination of defilements. What situations tend to inflame your anger, conceit, selfishness, envy, self-pity, longing, or craving? In what situations do you tend to react with obsessive sensual desire, meanness, aversion, or other responses that lead to suffering? Consider how you relate to political conversations at family gatherings, gossip at a party, quarterly reviews at work, an unexpected encounter with an ex-lover in the grocery store, smelling a cigarette or the aroma of freshly baked cookies, or the sight of someone stylishly dressed or heavily tattooed.

When you encounter a situation that challenges your equilibrium and you sense your mind is affected by desire or aversion, diligently curb your reactions. Otherwise, you might find your mind metaphorically grazing on the defilements. Like the cowherd who actively guides his cows, there are times when we must remain attentive and alert, prodding the mind to keep it from straying into areas that will produce suffering. Recognize the danger in a wandering mind and carefully watch what it grazes on.

This is not to suggest that all our thoughts are seething with defilement. Often we are just immersed in our own stories, plans, and problems, concerned with the responsibilities that structure our daily activities. Sometimes our thoughts concern our meditation practice, inspirations toward generosity, compassionate actions, reflections on virtue or Dhamma teachings. When the Buddha noticed that his thoughts were flavored by renunciation, lovingkindness, or compassion, he declared, "This does not lead to my own affliction, or to others' affliction, or to the affliction of both; it aids wisdom, does not cause difficulties, and leads to Nibbāna."[18]

There is nothing to fear from the many good, kind, wise, and useful thoughts you think each day. Regarding these, the Buddha commented, "Just as in the last month of the hot season, when all the crops have been brought inside the villages, a cowherd would guard his cows while staying at the root of a tree or out in the open, since he needs only to be mindful that the cows are there; so too, there was need for me only to be mindful that those states were there."[19]

The cowherd simile suggests a relaxed and gentle approach to being mindful of wholesome thoughts. When kind and wise thoughts are predominant, let yourself relax and gently watch your mind without interfering. In the simile, the cowherd simply sits in the shade of a tree and is mindful that his cows are there. You can simply be mindful that wholesome thoughts are arising in your mind.

By allowing wholesome thoughts to be there, you can develop numerous beautiful qualities that support spiritual growth. When you feel joyful appreciation upon watching children play with their friends, allow yourself to delight in the recognition that loving-kindness is manifesting in your neighborhood. When a colleague is rewarded for an achievement and, instead of harboring envy, you think "Congratulations! Good for you! Well done!"—trust these joyful thoughts. They support a healthy relationship that is not corrupted by envy. When the inspiration to donate to charity or give a gift to a friend pops into your mind, do not abandon the thought—act on it! Then, notice the joy that comes with being generous.

Behaviors, thoughts, and habits are reinforced by the rewards that we gain from the actions.[20] By noticing the unpleasant contraction, agitation, and anger that accompany envy and stinginess and comparing it to the expansiveness, ease, and delight that occur when we rejoice and are generous, the mind can revise the reward value it associates with these actions. When we recognize the benefits that wholesome actions produce, we tend to favor those actions in the future.[21]

Some thoughts serve as reminders to be mindful of our values. When a coworker urges you to sign off on a padded expense report so that both of you financially benefit, pay attention to that feeling of being dirtied by the suggestion. That feeling tells you that you will be happier if you choose the virtue of restraint.

Practice being gentle, even with wholesome thoughts. When a thought to help your neighbor arises, you should neither actively dispel the thought nor obsessively plan how you will help, but trust that this good intention will draw you into appropriate action at a suitable time. You do not need to spend your meditation time dwelling on it or lie awake at night plotting ways to help. When beautiful thoughts arise in your mind during meditation, you don't need to vigorously poke and prod them to go away! You should not, however, feed them with more restless thinking.

 WAIT

A popular acronym for improving communication skills is WAIT.

Ask yourself: Why Am I Talking?

By pausing to ask yourself this question, you can clarify the intentions that guide your verbal interactions. You may also try a variation on WAIT—Why Am I Thinking? Let this inquiry expose the internal forces that fuel your distractions.

By skillfully inclining your mind away from unwholesome thoughts and toward wholesome ones, you are encouraging wise action and building a strong foundation for spiritual development. The Buddha taught, "Abandon what is unwholesome and devote yourself to wholesome states, for that is how you will come to growth, increase, and fulfillment."[22]

A remarkable quality of mental peace can pervade experience when we are dedicated to abandoning unwholesome states and cultivating wholesome states. Supported by clearly wholesome intentions, we can stand firm on our own feet in conversations and interactions, in solitude and silence, free from remorse, worry, and regret. When we trust our intentions, whatever we do will occur with clarity and wisdom. Throughout the day, observe your intentions: from the motivation that nurtures your meditation practice to your interactions, conversations, or work.

The Buddha was not born enlightened, but he did the work to purify his mind. He learned about his personal mental habits. He worked to remove harmful intentions and weaken the underlying fetters of sensual desire, ill will, and ignorance that nourish hurtful thoughts.

It might reassure you to know that even the great Buddha initially struggled with troublesome thoughts until the harmful mental habits gradually subsided and ceased. His greatness developed through the diligence of his practice—not luck, not fate, not a gift of grace. He reflected, learned about his own mind, and took the appropriate action by abandoning harmful thought patterns. By engaging in an honest and thorough exploration of his mind, the Buddha freed it from unwholesome entanglements. You can do the same for yourself.

Everyone has some work to do to transform the conditioned patterns of their minds. You may notice that chronic complaining cultivates irritation and anger. You might also discover that frequent thoughts of virtue enhance joy and trustworthiness. If the same hindrances are repeatedly arising, try to identify the patterns that feed those obstructive thoughts. You have the power to influence, to develop, and to train your mind. The Buddha did it, and you can do it.

Consider which wholesome states you might develop to produce conditions in which the hindrance would not easily arise. Over time and with diligent practice, the wholesome states rather than hindrances can become the tendencies of your mind.

The Intentional Pause

To observe the volitional impulse, notice the moment that precedes an action. We might call it the "about-to-move" or the "about-to-speak" impulse. Consider:

- What types of intentions are moving you toward this verbal or bodily action?
- What happens if you inhibit or let go of the intention (to scratch an itch, for example) and just stay still and simply rest in the awareness of sensations and feelings?
- What happens if you pause when you are about to launch into speech and commit to listening instead? Can you stop yourself from making that nasty remark and notice the state of your mind?
- Instead of speaking or acting, discover what fuels habitual patterns within your mind. Every time you recognize an intention rooted in craving, anger, or delusion, take a moment for a brief reflective pause. Refuse to let unhealthy patterns determine your actions.
- Explore mental actions as well, such as dwelling in planning fantasies that might occur as you perform routine activities like driving down the freeway.
- Which volitional attitudes sustain the wandering mind?
- What does restless thinking serve?
- Are you entertaining yourself, preparing yourself, passing the time, or reinforcing a self-image?
- Are the planning fantasies of the wandering mind related to worry, comparing, or confirming a sense of yourself?

INCLINING TOWARD STILLNESS

Wholesome thoughts, although preferable to unwholesome thoughts in many ways, can still distract the mind from the deep stillness of concentration. The Buddha observed,

> "'If I think and ponder upon this thought even for a night, even for a day, even for a night and a day, I see nothing to fear from it. But with excessive thinking and pondering I might tire my body, and when the body is tired, the mind becomes disturbed, and when the mind is disturbed, it is far from concentration.' So, I steadied my mind internally, quieted it, brought it to singleness, and concentrated it. Why is that? So that my mind should not be disturbed."[23]

Concentration develops when the mind settles and is not obsessed with either coarse or subtle, unwholesome or wholesome thoughts. When you have abandoned unwholesome thoughts and refrain from the myriad deluded stories about things you have done or imagine doing, when you are not swept away by the prattle of innocuous distractions, when you stop fueling even kind, beautiful thoughts—then concentration will deepen. Beyond the activities of thinking, a still mind can be deeply healing and profoundly freeing.

SUMMARY OF MAIN POINTS

Intentions are thoughts that lead to actions. Repeated thoughts affect our dispositional traits, condition how we experience life, and increase the likelihood that similar thoughts will arise again.

The Buddha divided his thoughts into two classes. He recognized that thoughts of sensual desire, ill will, and cruelty cause affliction, whereas intentions toward renunciation, kindness, and compassion do not cause affliction. Wholesome thoughts tend to produce happiness; unwholesome thoughts tend to produce agitation.

Wholesome thoughts may be beneficial in daily life, but the aim of the Buddha's teachings goes beyond cultivating a kind and gentle quality of daily living. By allowing all thoughts, wholesome as well as unwholesome, to settle through meditation, you can reap the benefits of an undistracted, still mind.

CHAPTER 3

ANTIDOTES AND ALTERNATIVES

*Strategy #1—Replace Unwholesome Thoughts
with Wholesome Thoughts*

*When they give attention to some other sign connected with
what is wholesome, then any evil unwholesome thoughts
connected with desire, with hate, and with delusion are
abandoned in them and subside.*
—MIDDLE LENGTH DISCOURSES OF THE BUDDHA[24]

THERE'S AN EXPERIENCE common to nearly all meditators. We sit down fully intending to be aware of our present
experience, and suddenly we are confronted with a cascade
of thoughts. We're assailed by worries, fantasies, imaginary arguments, or planning what we are going to do later.

What do you do when this happens to you? Do you pass judgment
on your meditative abilities? Do you get lost in a self-created dream
world? Do you spend your meditation period turning thoughts over
and over in your mind? Do you end the meditation session, figuring
this isn't a good time to sit?

In the previous chapter, we distinguished between wholesome and unwholesome thoughts, noticing the kinds of mental activities that tend to lead to happiness and those that tend to lead to harm. The simple recognition of an unwholesome thought process might be sufficient for some unwholesome thoughts to subside. Still, if you have noticed a recurring pattern of thought, you might need to employ a fuller array of strategies to neutralize these pesky habitual thoughts.

This chapter begins our exploration of the five strategies that the Buddha taught in the discourse, the Removal of Distracting Thoughts:

> Replacing
> Examining
> Ignoring
> Investigating
> Resolving[25]

We create habits by repeating a thought or action over and over again. By using a similar method, you can change your habits and reinforce more skillful patterns. Once you have gained enough insight to recognize the unwholesome thoughts that create stress in your life, they lose their grip on your mind.

The series of strategies we will explore in the remainder of this book can be used to intervene in thought processes that are rooted in the three poisons—lust, hatred, and delusion.

The first strategy requires that we recognize when unwholesome thoughts of lust, hate, and delusion have overtaken the mind and then make an effort to replace them with wholesome alternatives. When we cultivate the ability to replace harmful thoughts with beneficial ones, we skillfully habituate the mind to a healthier thought pattern. You can opt to cultivate kindness, gratitude, patience, and wisdom rather than indulge defilements, and you can build new patterns that infuse your mind with joy, wisdom, and inspiration instead of lust, hate, and delusion.

Look carefully and honestly at defilements that arise in your own mind and give yourself the opportunity to select better alternatives. You can do this by moving your attention from unwholesome thought patterns to wholesome ones, as the Buddha instructed: "When a bhikkhu is giving attention to some sign, and owing to that sign, there arise in him evil, unwholesome thoughts connected with desire, with hate, and with delusion, then he should give attention to some other sign connected with what is wholesome."[26]

FLEXIBILITY OF PERCEPTION: SKILL WITH SIGNS

This first approach develops flexibility with perception. Before we can intelligently apply flexibility, we must understand how our perception functions. Perception involves the comprehension of what are called *signs*. The word *sign* in the above quote refers to any aspect of the object that you are noticing. This can be in the form of the color of a visible sight, shrillness of a sound, throbbing of a sensation, fear associated with a memory, the word or name that labels it, or the recognition of any aspect of experience.

Each day, you are bombarded with stimuli, which your mind organizes into perceptions. These perceptions are limited by what you already know and by biases that predate the present encounter. It would be exhausting to meet experience without the aid of preexisting information that helps to frame and interpret the experience. For example, you might recognize that this is a book (or ebook) by comparing a cluster of associated signs with the memory of previous encounters you have had with similar objects. This particular book may be new to you, but because you see a narrow rectangular shape—composed of paper, bound together on one side and sporting lines of printed words—and you picked it off a bookshelf, you can recognize this as a book.

Signs are not only the words or labels we assign to the object, such as the word *book*. They are also the sensory or mental impressions that are used to construct perceptions. Signs make it possible to perceive and interpret the world, though these perceptions and interpretations may not always be accurate.

People are quick to judge others based on signs of wealth, status, style, or power. Gender, hairstyle, clothing brands, body shape, facial expressions and posture, or the type of transportation one uses are among the many signs commonly used to classify people. Each day you get dressed and walk out of your home, you are flashing signs of your social position, personality, and political or religious affiliations. Others interpret those signs and place you into their preconceived, mentally constructed social structure. You also solidify a sense of yourself by identifying with the signs that help you fit into certain social groups and distinguish yourself from others.

Understanding how your perceptions are created gives you the power to alter them. If you notice that your interpretation of an object triggers greed, aversion, or delusion, then you might intentionally try to see it from a different perspective. Look at something else, or consciously shift from the aspect that habitually catches your attention to a different facet of the experience.

For example, suppose you saw a book with a 1950s cartoon on the cover and immediately thought, "I'm not interested in that." You could notice the judgmental reaction, your identification with generationally conditioned tastes, and opt to move closer to the book anyway. You might examine the colors in the cover image; you might feel the texture of the paper; you might open the book and scan the table of contents. Perhaps your initially negative judgment might make way for a new thought: "I wonder what this book is about?"

One meditation practitioner noticed that in the last ten minutes of using her exercise bike, she would frequently think about annoying things her husband had done. As she became aware of this pattern, she realized that when she was pushing herself hard in her workout and feeling the unpleasant sensations from the intense exercise, her mind gravitated toward more unpleasant thoughts.

She watched her mind conjuring up alternative explanations for the unpleasant feelings and searching for scapegoats to blame for her tiredness. By simply paying attention to her present sensations, feelings, and thoughts, she could accept her experience as tiredness, and her husband no longer caught the blame. Her mindfulness of feeling tiredness replaced the habit of blame.

By becoming mindful of the aspects of the world around us that we give our attention to, we can be flexible and change the focus of attention. We may not have control over everything in our environment, but by learning to shift our attention, we avoid getting stuck in unhealthy, unwholesome, or unhelpful ways of perceiving.

For example, when you attend a class, are you listening to the lecture, reading enticing messages on your cellphone, watching an attractive person, worrying about the next exam, or noticing dirt on your shoe? Your experience of the class is defined by what occupies your attention. Mindfulness will refine the way that you meet, attend to, and perceive experiences.

As you develop mindfulness, you will cultivate a more refined degree of skill in signs. The mastery of signs that develops through meditation will inform how you interpret, interact with, and relate to every conscious moment. It will affect the clarity and suitability of your comprehension of experience. Without this competency, it would be impossible to distinguish wholesome from unwholesome options. By developing skill in signs, you will learn to notice which ones your senses pick up on and how your mind weaves them into coherent perceptions.

Meditative awareness clarifies (1) what you give your attention to, (2) the quality of that attention, and (3) how effective the attention is. Are you attending to experience in a useful and wise way? Or is your attention carelessly increasing your entanglement in unwholesome states?

✎⊱ *Shifting Signs*

Notice how you attend to ordinary perceptions and allow some flexibility in altering the signs that you pick up on. For example, there are many varied signs that you can focus on when looking at a bowl of cherries. Some ways of viewing the cherries could entangle the mind in sensual craving as you unmindfully consume the fruit.

Another way of seeing could lead to possessiveness as you plan where to plant a cherry tree. Or you could focus on the color and find that the color triggers myriad associations. Other ways of viewing those same cherries could support contemplating nutriment, impermanence, and gratitude for the food. How you see something affects whether the perception will be supportive or detrimental to your mental balance, clarity, and wisdom.

When your mind is unduly obsessed with gaining a sensual pleasure, such as the luscious taste of a cherry, notice more than the object that you want; notice what you see in it that is triggering repeated thoughts of desire.

- ► Do you imagine getting a pleasant feeling from it?
- ► Do you anticipate a sense of security, comfort, power, or control?
- ► Are you enchanted by the color, shape, aroma, or idea?
- ► Are you trying to repeat a similar experience from the past?
- ► Do you envision someone seeing you with it?
- ► What triggers or fuels this craving?

Once you become aware of the sign that has attracted your attention, replace that perception with something less alluring about it. For example, if you are attracted to the taste, consider the calorie count. If you are drawn in by the smell, contemplate it rotting. If you are fascinated by the idea of owning it, consider that it will not last.

Develop the flexibility of attention that will allow you to shift the signs, even as you reach for, pick up, and eat those cherries.

KNOCKING OUT DISTRACTING THOUGHTS

A traditional simile in the Pāli Canon is that of a carpenter who uses a smaller peg to dislodge a larger peg in a block of wood. When the larger peg is dislodged, the smaller one doesn't stay stuck in the hole left in the wood. If you feel caught up in a familiar mental drama, it might help just to think about something else for a moment. Try to replace the harmful mental habit with an inspiring or positive thought. Like the small peg, the new thought will not get stuck.

When a friend moved to a new city, she was initially enchanted with the charm of its neighborhoods: adorable cottage-style homes, window boxes overflowing with red geraniums and blue lobelia, front porches with swings, and towering conifers providing shelter to squirrels and birds. These features would delight her on her daily walks. But as the months and years went by, habitual everyday worries began to overshadow the simple enjoyment of the neighborhoods around her, so she intentionally decided to once again stimulate delight in her surroundings. She looked at a vibrant window box, focused on the colors, and appreciated the careful tending that was given to the plants.

At first resistance arose, accompanied by subtle negative

thoughts: "Yeah, that may be beautiful, but life is dreary and hard and I have this and that to attend to." Still, every second or two, she deliberately brought her attention back to present delightful signs—a squirrel enthusiastically nibbled a nut, children giggled as they scooted past on tricycles, an ant carried a small seed across the sidewalk, a rose emitted a fragrant aroma, a neighbor tended his garden, drivers of two passing cars paused on the road to exchange greetings, and she felt a pleasant bounce in her step.

At first, her mental gloom persisted. But little by little, by diligently replacing habitual worries with simple perceptions of ordinary things, she was reminded that gloomy mental habits are not the whole of reality, and joy returned.

At the most basic level, meditation practice is your laboratory for learning to notice and then replace unwholesome thoughts with wholesome ones. By recognizing restlessness, you can choose to restore mindfulness. You can train your mind to let go of one thing and replace it with another. This is the most common corrective employed in meditation. Simply by focusing on your meditation object, such as returning your attention to the present experience of sitting and breathing whenever you are lost in a story, you can replace restlessness with steady attention.

When you let go of distracting personal narratives, you weaken the underlying defilement of conceit and replace it with renunciation. By bringing your attention to the sensations of sitting and breathing during meditation, you let go of the enchantment with thoughts. That's what it means to replace the unwholesome with the wholesome. It is a simple way of tidying up the mind. When thoughts arise, be mindful that they have arisen, and gently sweep them aside.

The parallel version of this discourse found in the Madhyama Āgama offers a variation on the carpentry simile. Rather than removing a peg, the simile suggests, "It is just as a carpenter or a carpenter's apprentice might apply an inked string to a piece of wood [to mark a straight line], and then trim the wood with a sharp adze to make it straight. In the same way, because the [preliminary] sign [has led to the arising of unwholesome thoughts], the monk instead attends to a different sign related to what is wholesome so that evil and unwholesome thoughts will no longer arise."[27]

Just as the carpenter uses a guide to systematically trim off uneven, jagged, and rough parts of the wood until the piece of wood is straight, meditators can consciously abandon thoughts that are crooked, rough, askew, or not aligned with virtue and their goals. You can intentionally extricate thoughts that are detrimental, and through this skillful removal, produce a wholesome, upright, clear mind.

ANTIDOTES AND ALTERNATIVES

Meditators learn to abandon habitual entanglement with the content of thoughts and direct attention to something more useful. By doing this, it is possible to clear the mind of compulsive clutter. Take the time to clear away fantasies about the future, ruminations about the past, and commentary about the present. By letting go of these habitual thoughts, you will become more attentive and present. Thoughts still arise in the course of meditation, but you learn not to be seduced by them. Notice their occurrence, abandon any attachment to them, and focus your energies in ways that support your goals.

Introduction to mindfulness classes often include the instruction to put mindfulness to work in everyday life. One meditator I know took up the challenge of working with the feelings of impatience that frequently arose when she was stopped at a red traffic signal. Instead of interpreting the round red light as an emphatic order to stop and wait, she began seeing it as a rich red heart whose glow reminded her to take that time to rest in mindfulness of the present moment. This practice virtually eliminated her impatience at stop signals.

First, you must identify the harmful thought process you wish to uproot and then wisely bring a useful antidote to counter it. For example, if you think that you are not worthy enough to practice the Buddha's noble teachings, replace that self-sabotaging thought with a commitment to try your best to practice virtue, develop mindfulness, and apply whatever degree of wisdom is accessible in your actions.

If you find yourself comparing your degree of concentration with an ideal of mastery, don't allow the comparing mind to discourage you or conclude that you are hopeless at meditation practice. Replace that negative assessment with a recognition of your capacity to grow, the joy you find in practice, and your good intentions.

One meditator shared how she used this strategy:

> I have a habit of viewing my partner like a princess, and not in a good way. I see her as someone who believes she is entitled to superior treatment and who will prioritize her own comfort over mine. Recently she brought my attention to the damage this view was doing to our relationship, and I agreed with her. I resolved that I would not indulge this view any longer. I decided that any time this view arose, I would abandon it and find an alternate view.
>
> Soon enough an opportunity arose to test my resolve. She asked me to go with her to the bike shop. The habitual thought began. This is for her convenience. She doesn't care what my priorities are for today. I recognized this as "the princess view" and abandoned it, replacing it with: how nice that she desires my company!
>
> The reward was immediate. I felt ease and spaciousness, in contrast to the pressure and irritation that would always accompany the princess view. The new thought dramatically improved my attitude, and I joined her at the bike shop without resentment.

Some readers might resist this approach, assuming it will enforce an artificially positive attitude, prevent the unbiased acceptance of conditions that would lead to wisdom, condemn certain emotions, or impose rigid religious values on the contents of our private thoughts. This practice, however, is not intended to amplify personal guilt or compel meditators to choose their thoughts from a prescreened list of authorized Buddhist ideals.

Instead, it is a means for dislodging harmful habitual patterns and freeing the mind for more creative, useful, and liberating pursuits. Honest reflection on your thoughts will help you differentiate between unhelpful thoughts and appropriate thoughts.

For example, painful feelings of grief can be accepted and felt. After a loved one has died, we do not use this strategy to replace sad thoughts with unrelated happy thoughts. Instead, with a balanced mind, we can allow the heart to grieve. This strategy should not artificially constrict the range of your thoughts; it simply shifts those patterns that reinforce harmful states toward thoughts that nourish beneficial states. In the case of grief, you might gradually let go of the attachment to your loved one's presence, and instead appreciate what you shared. Rather than dwell in angry stories about love you have lost, feel the physical sensations and emotional feelings that appear as waves of grief arise, wash over you, and then pass away.

For the replacement strategy to be effective, you must choose the alternative wisely. Be careful not to replace comparing thoughts with other types of restless or aversive thoughts, such as jealous expectations or petty faultfinding. Learn to shift from the unwholesome to the wholesome. This shift requires the ability to distinguish between beneficial thoughts and detrimental thoughts. It can be as simple as replacing self-sabotaging views with a joyful appreciation of whatever you are actually mindful of in the present moment.

Once I had a student who was preoccupied with violent hateful thoughts. He figured that since sexual fantasies felt lighter than his hate-filled thoughts, he would replace hate with lust. This approach only further agitated his mind—he was adding a second hindrance on top of the first.

Another student confessed that because angry thoughts quickly raised her energy, she intentionally thought about people who had hurt her to leverage the accompanying anger when she felt slothful during meditation. But since her mind was inclined toward dullness, she did not have the energetic resources to dispel the anger, and the agitation rapidly increased and developed into rage. The Buddha did not recommend multiplying the hindrances!

CHANGING HABITS

You might also use this strategy of replacement to work with habitual actions, by noticing a habitual activity that is not healthy for you, removing it, and replacing it with something better.

For example, you might have a habit of waking up in the morning and lingering in bed, listening to the morning news, but find that you are starting each day feeling grumpy. When you are groggy, it may be difficult to protect your mind. You might change that habit to begin your day with loving-kindness practice, and postpone listening to the news until enough mindfulness is established that you can consider world affairs without being thrown off balance.

Another meditator tended to ramp up the planning mind, even before getting out of bed in the morning. Her mind would anticipate the many responsibilities, meetings, and important activities that she had scheduled for that day. She mentally rehearsed the details of how her day would unfold. Sometimes she would even imagine herself feeling exhausted by her busy schedule.

Powering through life can feel exciting, but also stressful. Although she believed these morning rehearsals supported her hard-won success, she saw that it was taking a toll on her moods and family relationships. She began to suspect that her morning planning frenzies were having unwanted effects, making her inconsiderate of her spouse, less patient with minor delays, more irritable with equipment failures, and intolerant of errors by colleagues.

She decided to experiment with intentionally slowing down the train of her thought to reduce her mental busyness. She maintained the same workload, but each morning when the habit of mentally rehearsing her busy day began to rev up, she chose to set it aside. Instead, she reflected on her values, which fostered calmness, clarity, and patience. She brought thoughts of family members to mind and focused on the qualities that she appreciated and loved in them. She chose to start her days by reading a poem or inspiring passages from a book that she enjoyed. She realized that she did not need to plan a vacation to envision the experience of relaxation. She discovered the joys of calmly starting each day and practiced being mindful and at ease while performing her work.

Does chronic worry affect your life? A meditator once described to me her experience of emerging from sleep each morning feeling aches, pains, and stiffness. She noticed that these sensations frequently triggered a stream of fearful thoughts even before she got out of bed. No matter how peaceful her life felt, her mind would conjure up things to worry about.

In the springtime she might obsess about whether she had gotten behind in planting her vegetable garden. Wasn't it long past time that the broccoli starts should go out? Shouldn't the tomato seedlings be under grow lights by now? Wouldn't the peas soon need a trellis? This backyard garden hobby assumed a life-or-death importance in her mind during the early morning hours, when her muscles felt sore and contracted. Around holidays she might have obsessive thoughts about who would attend family gatherings or how various cousins were living their lives.

She began to work with this by reciting phrases of goodwill toward herself. Starting the day with thoughts of goodwill while still in bed, performing a few gentle stretches, and then sitting up for a brief meditation successfully quelled those worry-fueled, early-morning thought rampages.

It is widely believed that stress is harmful, and plenty of research on the effects of stress on health has been conducted in recent decades. Beliefs have a powerful impact on how we respond to potential stressors. Interestingly, research has shown that if we believe that stress is bad for our health, that belief itself is a significant indicator of our risk of dying of a stress-related illness.[28]

What we habitually think about has an enormous effect on our lives, health, relationships, activities, and sense of potential. We all face challenging conditions in life, but their ability to damage our mental and physical health is influenced by how we think. Our beliefs during times of stress can intensify stressful events and amplify the harmful effects.

Stress affects the bodies, emotions, and minds of people differently. When studying the stress response, researchers found that people who seem to manage stress well were physically aroused to respond; their blood pressure increased, but they didn't interpret the event as stressful, so the body settled back to normalcy.[29] People who perceive a situation as a challenge tend to mobilize themselves to overcome the obstacle and achieve their goal. Someone who focuses on the stress of the situation, on the other hand, could easily be capsized by it.

A healthy stress response can be likened to a deer who runs when alerted to danger, but after the threat has passed returns to peaceful grazing. The next time you are in a stressful situation, such as when you are running late, find a leaking water pipe in your home, or stand up to speak in public, try inserting the thought that your stress response is preparing your body and mind to effectively deal with the threat. Let that thought support confidence in your ability to handle the situation. Then let the thinking go, relax the mind, and return your attention to the present activity that you are engaged in.

By developing healthy alternatives, you gradually change the disposition of your own tendencies.

COUNTERING THE HINDRANCES

Five classic hindrances are taught in the Buddhist tradition: sensual desire, anger or aversion, sloth and torpor, restlessness and remorse, and doubt. These hindrances often manifest through reactive thoughts and obstruct the cultivation of concentration and wisdom.

Mindfulness is a universal antidote that can dispel all the hindrances. When we are mindful, we are not compelled to blindly repeat conditioned patterns. But when the continuity of our mindfulness is weak, hindrances are more likely to arise. Although any hindrance can be banished by restoring mindfulness and skillfully directing your attention, each hindrance is also paired with specific traditional antidotes.

The antidotes mentioned below will support the development of your mindfulness while simultaneously replacing the unwholesome hindrance with a wiser alternative.

Lust and Thoughts of Sensual Desire

If the mind is entangled with sensual thoughts, first recognize that this is a hindrance to your peace of mind. Notice that you are perceiving something or someone in a way that is enticing. Then ask yourself, what might be another way of seeing this?

A classic substitution recommended to celibate monastics is to see bodies as not beautiful. The Pāli term *asubha* means "not-beautiful" or "foul." When appropriately practiced, asubha reflections produce a balanced, equanimous mind, with insights into the functioning of perception. Meditators who find that lust is a dominant hindrance—regardless of whether they are lay practitioners or monastics—might benefit from these asubha practices.

As you walk down the street noticing the shape, clothing, and features of the people who pass by, you might perceive someone as attractive, and your mind might float off into romantic fantasies. Someone else might appear repugnant, and judgmental thoughts might dominate the narrative. These interpretations can develop into stories of passion, rumination, anxiety, and worry. All you really see, however, are the colors of clothing, head hairs, body hairs, nails, teeth, skin.

When you consider bodies as composed of anatomical parts, lust will not readily arise. The asubha practices can be developed further by contemplating the internal parts or impurities of bodies. Skin only appears beautiful when we ignore the fact that this layer of dead cells is continuously flaking off the body, leaving a trail of sediment in the wake of movement. Bodies ooze, stink when not washed, and harbor bacteria. Your own body and the bodies of others will weaken with age, fall ill, inevitably die, and eventually decay. Yet, the fact that bodies age, become ill, and decay rarely features in romantic fantasies.

There may be times in our lives when it could be useful to perceive things as *not-beautiful*. If you are attracted to someone with whom it would be harmful to yourself or others to pursue a relationship, choose to be aware that this is simply a body, a material form. Suspend the habit of interpreting the bodily shape, flow of the hair, color of the skin, pattern of the gait, the texture of the lips, or the tone of the muscles as signs of beauty. See them only as signs of matter or as a collection of anatomical parts—not inherently attractive.

This approach provides a method for perceiving bodies with equanimity—as natural, material processes. All matter shares characteristics of color, shape, smell, hardness, heat. To become engrossed in craving, lost in possessiveness, and distracted by greedy desires, you must first misperceive the object and see it through the lens of lust. Beauty is not inherent in the form that is seen; it is constructed by the mind and influenced by personal and cultural associations. For example, leanness is considered beautiful in some cultures, while other cultures favor obesity.

By recognizing the way we construct the sign of beauty and invest power in it, fantasies of sensual lust appear less compelling. Meditators train their minds to appreciate virtuous qualities and enjoy present pleasant feelings, while not grasping the signs of beauty that might engross the mind in fantasy.

Asubha practice should not create hatred or fear of sensual experiences; instead, it is a practice of shifting the sign. Asubha practice does not result in a joyless, drab existence. It succeeds by deterring perception from interpreting signs in ways that lead to possessiveness, identification, and unhealthy entanglement.

If you are aware that a great deal of your attention is engrossed in sensual desires, don't wait for the next attack of lust to do something about it. Meditators with a strong disposition toward lust might benefit by cultivating qualities that can prevent its arising. For example, a daily reflection on the virtue of generosity or conditions that bring you gratitude can shift tendencies from lustful desire toward contentment. Actively nourish states of gratitude, appreciation, and happiness with what you have already. Proactively incline your mind toward the joy of letting go rather than attachment.

Ill Will, Anger, Aversion

The classic antidote to ill will is loving-kindness: when goodwill is present, anger is absent. When you notice irritated, impatient, judgmental, or angry thoughts, shift to thoughts of friendliness, compassion, or kindness.

One meditation student became aware that he frequently found his coworkers irritating. He often noticed behaviors that triggered angry thoughts. To shift this pattern, he intentionally noticed qualities that he respected and appreciated in his colleagues. Those irritable moods softened and soon melted away, and he found that his work relationships became friendlier and more productive.

If you have a strong disposition toward anger and hatred, you might make goodwill a feature of your daily meditation practice. Each time you encounter somebody who annoys you, try to contemplate one quality that you respect or appreciate. Don't let your mind build a moment of aversion into a lingering story of hatred. Just notice that alongside some annoying qualities there are also qualities worthy of admiration. This wholesome perspective allows you to recognize in others positive qualities that might have been otherwise obstructed by your negative view.

Watch your mind. When it strays into an aversive state during meditation, work, or just a chat with a friend, shift your attention to a beneficial thought. At the beginning of your daily meditation practice, you might take a few minutes to nurture goodwill by reciting phrases such as "may we be happy, may we be well, may we live with ease" silently in your mind. When you train the mind to shift responsively and responsibly, you stop allowing anger to dominate your view.

Sometimes people get irritated with the ones they love most dearly, live close to, or respect highly. When you feel angry at your spouse, partner, sibling, or friend, notice whether your attention is riveted to negative views about their character. To counteract these thought processes, make a list of the person's positive qualities. When you feel trapped in anger, you can take out your list and review it. Notice how you feel when you are caught up in anger, and notice how you feel when you contemplate their positive qualities. Allow yourself to marvel at your good fortune to know someone like this—perhaps in less irritated moments you consider this person to be fun, talented, loyal, intelligent, caring, helpful, generous, spiritual.

If you find yourself trying to appreciate your friend's beautiful qualities, but your mind justifies your anger and refuses to let go of the feelings of irritation, relax and continue to recall their good qualities. Persistence can shift the focus of your attention and chip away at any negative feelings you have built up. This exercise will not change your friend's unique blend of character traits, but it can free your mind from dwelling on the irritating ones, thereby providing a balanced view and appreciation for the whole person.

Sloth and Torpor

The hindrance of sloth and torpor is not mere physical fatigue or sleepiness; sloth and torpor arise when you cannot apply enough energy or interest to be present with your experience. It is primarily a failure of attention.

The obvious antidote to sloth and torpor is to increase energy. When you feel dull during meditation, you might open your eyes to let light in; perk up your interest; recall your purpose; or physically stand up, stretch, and do some walking meditation. A reflection on death can instill a sense of urgency and inspire you to use your limited time and resources wisely. Remembering your aim, sensing the subtle joy of being present, and activating curiosity can restore your energy.

When your mind feels dull and disinterested in the present experience, you might remind yourself that you choose to be here—surely you do not want to miss your life through dullness and inattention.

Getting interested in your experience requires curiosity, which is both energizing and rewarding. Give yourself a pep talk. Encourage yourself not to resist whatever is present right now; relax into present-moment awareness.

Restlessness and Remorse

Restlessness might be the most common and persistent of the hindrances. It accompanies all the other hindrances and can arise as either physical or mental agitation. You might recognize it in the impulse to glance at your watch during meditation. You might see it manifest when you frequently check your phone for messages. A craving for entertaining stimulation or discontent with the quietude of a Sunday afternoon may reveal an undercurrent of restlessness.

Your foot impatiently tapping during a conversation might be a signal to notice agitated boredom. Most habitual trains of thought could be categorized as restless thoughts.

Remorse is traditionally mentioned as a specific type of restlessness. It is sometimes described as worry and is accompanied by aversion. It manifests as ruminations about past actions, regret over mistakes or missed opportunities, or fear about potential outcomes.

To overcome restlessness, worry, and remorse, we must learn to calm, concentrate, and settle the mind. When the mind or body is agitated, we might invite a calm presence by asking the question "Can I be still with this?" And then gently turn your attention to meet the agitation, restlessness, or worry without embellishing it. I have asked myself this question many times, and I nearly always answer "Yes, of course I can be still with this" and genuinely sense calm interest supporting my present experience. Nevertheless, I like to phrase it as an inquiry to keep my options open and repeatedly rediscover that I have the ability to meet the present moment as it is. Here, curiosity replaces resistance, calmness replaces restlessness, and confidence replaces worry.

But you might wonder what a meditator would do if the answer is "No, I can't be with this, not even for this one moment!" This might happen when there is extreme exhaustion, and you cannot muster up the energy to be attentive, or when you are facing a particularly traumatic event. In these cases, you might jump to the third strategy, which will be discussed in chapter 5—skillful distraction.

Doubt

When you do not understand your experience clearly, speculative thinking accelerates, and doubt festers. Thus, careful attention is the primary antidote to the hindrance of doubt. Doubt ends by understanding for yourself the kind of action that leads to happiness and the kind that leads to harm. When you know something for yourself, you won't have any doubts about it.

Doubt cannot develop when you meet experience with continuous mindfulness or clear discernment. By cultivating mindfulness of your own mind, doubt will not gain a foothold. When you can clearly identify what is beneficial and what is detrimental, doubt will not be able to corrupt your view.

If doubt is one of your common hindrances and wisdom is elusive, you might reflect daily on your virtues or the inspiring qualities of the Buddha. Refresh your own capacity to learn and grow in the spiritual life by reflecting on a feeling of peace or joy that you have experienced in meditation, a flash of insight that occurred sometime in your practice, or a moment when you refrained from causing harm.

Mindful Inquiry Is the Universal Antidote

It is not always necessary to formulate a unique and individual response for every restless, deluded, or confused thought. Often by the time that you have noticed that you are distracted, the thoughts have slipped away. You may or may not recall what you were thinking about four seconds earlier. Let those wispy thoughts simply fade away.

Whenever you realize that you are lost in thought, you have the option to return to mindfulness of the present moment or reconnect with your meditation object. When you intentionally let go of a thought, find that the thought vanishes when you realize you are thinking, or discover that thoughts settle naturally, you can return to mindful awareness. You have essentially replaced the unwholesome state of restlessness, doubt, or delusion with the wholesome state of mindfulness.

Because habits are often entrenched, it is helpful to prepare in advance by composing several possible replacement options for each of your common hindrances. For example, if you find yourself engaged in self-criticism, you might routinely ask yourself the question, "Is this really true in all situations?" If you tend to disparage yourself with thoughts—"I can't do this. I'm no good. I'll never be as good as somebody else."—then remind yourself of three of your own wonderful qualities.

✿ Prepare Alternatives in Advance

On a piece of paper, jot down three thoughts or unhealthy beliefs that frequently arise in your mind. For each of these three unwholesome thoughts, propose a few possible positive replacement thoughts. Try them out throughout the day and see which might serve as effective antidotes to the entrenched negative patterns. By predetermining replacement options, you will have tools handy when you need them. Whenever a harmful thought arises, you can quickly replace it with a better alternative.

If you distract yourself by composing lists during your daily sitting meditation, then try reminding yourself to feel the present physical sensations in your hands and feet, noticing how these sensations change. If you notice yourself thinking "I'll never be able to meditate," let go of future attainments and appreciate becoming mindful of that worry right now.

Try replacing anxious planning with a calm reassurance that this moment is OK just as it is. Try replacing irritated comments with thoughts of appreciation. Try replacing sexual lust with a reflection that bodies are composed of hair, teeth, nails, and skin. Whenever the mind is caught up in an opinion or lost in a reaction of desire, aversion, or delusion, ask yourself, "Is there another way of seeing this?"

You can be creative and develop your own personalized antidotes.

You do not need to be trapped by habitual thoughts. Thoughts are impermanent and always changing. When they are understood as discrete mental events that arise and pass away, they do not cause much turbulence. By developing the ability to replace one thought, sign, or perception with an alternative, you confirm that these are not fixed characteristics of who you are. Developing the strategy of replacing loosens attachment to your habitual mode of viewing yourself. When you are not rigidly identified with thoughts, your ability to direct your mind as you choose will grow stronger. When the wisdom of non-identification thoroughly replaces old habits of clinging, profound freedom of mind will pervade all your encounters.

SUMMARY OF MAIN POINTS

Is your way of perceiving and thinking about life leading to happiness, or is it perpetuating suffering? This strategy of replacing encourages you to shift how your experience is perceived. To prevent unwholesome thoughts from inhibiting your capacity to be genuinely present for life, practice replacing harmful thoughts with more skillful alternatives.

Sometimes, just recognizing that a thought isn't helping us produces sufficient clarity that it ceases. If not, you may cultivate this first strategy by replacing the thought with a wholesome alternative. This might be accomplished by returning attention to the meditation object, favoring a purposeful and positive thought, or shifting your perspective toward a kinder viewpoint.

The strategy of replacement is a classic method for addressing hindrances when they arise. Harmful, obsessive, or distracting sensual desires can be overcome by contemplating the unattractive properties of whatever is desired. Ill will can be replaced with goodwill; dullness, with energetic commitment; restlessness, with calmness; and doubt, with the confidence that results from careful attention.

⁀⊚ *Replacing Thoughts*

After recognizing unwholesome thoughts as unwholesome, choose to channel your mental energies in a more positive and refined direction. Try replacing the problematic thought pattern with a thought that is more skillful.

Choose a wholesome alternative. For example, don't replace anger with lust even if lust seems easier to bear. This exercise should not heap more hindrances on the mind. The strategy is to replace harmful thoughts with helpful thoughts.

Considering what you've learned about your own tendencies so far, choose an unwholesome pattern to work with this week—a kind of unwholesome thought that is likely to arise. Write out a few potential antidotes or alternatives that you could apply. For example, you might:

- ▸ Replace anger toward a colleague with a reflection on a quality that you appreciate about that person; think of their virtues.
- ▸ Replace worry by trusting your capacity to meet the present moment.
- ▸ Replace restlessness with your meditation object, take a few calm mindful breaths, or reflect on your commitment to clarity and calm.
- ▸ Decide not to indulge repetitive thoughts about fiction, TV, or movies, and ground your attention in present bodily sensations.

- ► If doubting thoughts erupt in the mind, remind yourself of what you value about this path.
- ► If controlling thoughts obsess your mind, remind yourself that things are OK as they are, that everything is impermanent and not under your control. Let it be enough to be mindful of what is.

Harmful beliefs and unexamined thoughts sustain many kinds of unhealthy habits. So, to successfully change your habits, begin by changing your thoughts.

CHAPTER 4

WEIGHING THE COSTS

Strategy #2—Examine the Dangers of
Distracting Thoughts

When one examines the danger in those thoughts, then any evil
unwholesome thoughts connected with desire, with hate, and with
delusion are abandoned in one and subside.
—MIDDLE LENGTH DISCOURSES OF THE BUDDHA[30]

IF REPLACING UNWHOLESOME thoughts with wholesome
ones as described in the previous chapter has calmed your distracted mind—great! You don't need to apply more strategies.
Simply continue developing your concentration, mindfulness, and
insight with your usual meditation practice. But if you find a persistent obsession or hindrance, try the next strategy in the training
sequence: examine the danger in that thought pattern.

The Buddha instructs,

> If . . . there still arise in him evil, unwholesome thoughts
> connected with desire, with hate and with delusion, then
> he should examine the danger in those thoughts thus:

> "These thoughts are unwholesome, they are reprehensible, they result in suffering." When he examines the danger in those thoughts, then any evil, unwholesome thoughts connected with desire, with hate and with delusion are abandoned in him and subside. With the abandoning of them his mind becomes steadied internally, quieted, brought to singleness, and concentrated.[31]

Here, the Buddha reminds us first that certain kinds of thoughts lead to suffering—those rooted in sensual desire, hate, and delusion. By comprehending the dangers that can come from these unwholesome thoughts, we will be motivated to disentangle our attachment to them. As the mind becomes freed from the burden of unwholesome thoughts, restlessness will settle, and concentration will improve.

CAN A THOUGHT BE DANGEROUS?

When examining the danger in a thought pattern, you might wonder how thoughts can be dangerous. Fantasies based in the desire for sensual pleasure might thwart the development of mindfulness by disconnecting you from your present experience. Preoccupation with aversion to a disagreeable event can cause you to feel irritable and to let anger affect your next encounter. Anger may then proliferate and create even more harm. When delusion is present, daydreams might dull your mind, causing you to miss emerging opportunities or adhere to biases that prevent clear seeing. When you are distracted by pleasurable fantasies, hate, or delusion, you are not cultivating mindfulness or developing your meditation.

How do you distinguish between an unwholesome thought process and a merely neutral mental activity? The key here is to consider both its roots and where they lead. Examine the thought closely to determine whether it is rooted in or leads to states that are infested with sensual desire, hate, or delusion. Notice whether your mental activities support the growth of wisdom and compassion or exacerbate anxiety, depression, or obsessive thinking.

For example, at first you might assume that there is nothing wrong with anticipating the pleasures of a celebratory outing to your favorite restaurant. But notice whether indulging thoughts laden with expectation heightens the clarity of your mind or leads to discontent. Does craving for future pleasure support the cultivation of compassion and insight, or does it distract you from being mindful and produce expectation that leads to future disappointment?

Restless thoughts might also appear innocuous, but notice how restlessness hinders the development of mindfulness. When mindfulness is weak, hindrances can flourish. Spending your meditation time planning daily activities might not seem evil, but when you are busy trying to control how future events will turn out, you overlook the impermanence of things. Examine your patterns and notice whether faultfinding, judgmental thoughts help you listen carefully to your spouse or friends or create discord in your relationships.

This investigation goes beyond identifying explicitly harmful thoughts. A thorough examination of the potential danger of thoughts will put even pleasant and innocuous thought patterns in the spotlight to determine if they, too, are leading you astray.

A Shocking Simile

We repeat habitual thought patterns that cause us suffering. We carry them around, clinging to them like emblems of who we are. The Buddha described them as being like ornaments and accessories—scarves, earrings, necklaces, bracelets, cufflinks—that people enjoy wearing. We dress up in these ornaments to display our identity and appear more attractive to others.

But dangerous thoughts are not just innocuous, shiny baubles. To illustrate the danger, the Buddha used the simile of someone draping themselves in the carcass of a snake, dog, or flayed human being. Imagine dressing in the morning and flinging the putrid corpse of a human being across your shoulder like a scarf or adorning yourself with the fresh, oozing carcass of a dog.

The fact that the Buddha chose such a graphic, shocking simile tells us something about the danger of being ignorant of the damage that can be caused by clinging to habitual, unwholesome thoughts. With a clear knowledge of the damage they do to us—in terms of our freedom and liberation—we would not wear them as innocuous baubles. We would see them as rotting carcasses and would be horrified to have them hanging from our bodies.

Reflecting on this simile, one student shared: "I had a juicy piece of gossip and was eager to share it with my husband. I felt proud to possess this morsel of news and looked forward to the laughter that would come with its telling. Then, this simile crossed my mind, and I realized with shock that I would have been wearing a corpse! This image highlighted how unskillful and hurtful it would have been to share the story—damaging for me, for my husband, and for the person I would have been gossiping about. Thankfully, the thought of the flayed corpse helped me to stop before I said anything."

CONSIDER THE CONSEQUENCES

To engage in careful examination, you must be bold enough to look starkly at the mind and see the treacherous consequences of indulging obsessions. Consider: when you entertained this pattern yesterday, how did it affect your mood? When you indulged this pattern last week, how did it affect your communication with your spouse? Notice where that line of thought leads. What pattern does it reinforce in your mind? Do you want to keep feeding that pattern?

You might reflect again on a message from the Buddha that we explored in chapter 2: "Whatever one frequently thinks and ponders upon, that will become the inclination of the mind."[32] Inquire deeply: Is this mental pattern increasing or decreasing your personal suffering and the suffering of those around you? After considering the consequences, do you still want to cultivate it?

Once you see that a thought pattern is harmful, perhaps those thoughts will simply vanish. On the other hand, you might be reluctant to let go. You might argue, "These thoughts are not as deluded as other thoughts I could be having. I am less deluded than other people." It might feel safer to maintain familiar patterns of body, speech, and mind even when you recognize that they are unwholesome.

But allowing habitual thoughts to overtake your mind has consequences. When you notice certain habitual thoughts creating trouble, pain, and conflict in your life, view those unwholesome thoughts as toxic. Stop making excuses for them. If you find your mind wants to avoid reflecting on the painful consequences of the habit and prefers to either berate you or dream about how different it can be in the future, gently guide your attention toward a realistic and balanced view of your situation. Don't just shrug your shoulders and allow habitual thoughts to run rampant through your mind. If you find that your mind constructs explanations or arguments to convince you to avoid change, examine the danger of clinging to familiar patterns. Out of respect for yourself and the virtues you have developed, recognize how even subtle habitual thoughts can hinder progress toward your personal, professional, and spiritual goals.

A friend's story from her youth demonstrates how, by seeing the harm certain patterns cause, we may be inspired to renounce them. As a young adult when casual romantic liaisons were very appealing, she entered into new relationships with abandon. At first it felt great, but after some time, the negative consequences of these pursuits became apparent. New romances fueled proliferating thoughts and fantasies that made it difficult to concentrate on her work. Some romances evolved into awkward, difficult-to-navigate relationships and triggered additional frenzies of distracting thoughts. Eventually, she decided to abandon the pursuit of casual romance. When someone new appeared attractive to her, she recalled the endpoints of previous casual romances and reflected on the mental agitation they produced. This was often enough to shift her attention toward nurturing stabler relationships.

The Fisherman's Hook

In the Saṃyutta Nikāya the Buddha describes a fisherman who casts a baited hook into the lake. An unwise fish might grasp the hook and meet with disaster. Why? Because the foolish fish focused on the bait's irresistible quality and failed to recognize the dangerous hook it concealed:

> Suppose a fisherman would cast a baited hook into a deep lake, and a fish on the lookout for food would swallow it. That fish who has thus swallowed the fisherman's hook would meet with calamity and disaster, and the fisherman could do with it as he wishes. So too, bhikkhus, there are these six hooks in the world for the calamity of beings, for the slaughter of living beings.
>
> There are, bhikkhus, forms cognizable by the eye that are desirable, lovely, agreeable, pleasing, sensually enticing, tantalizing. If a bhikkhu seeks delight in them, welcomes them, and remains holding to them, he is called a bhikkhu who has swallowed Mara's hook. He has met with calamity and disaster, and the Evil One can do with him as he wishes.
>
> There are, bhikkhus, sounds cognizable by the ear . . . [odors cognizable by the nose . . . flavors cognizable by the tongue . . . tangibles cognizable by the body . . .] mental phenomena cognizable by the mind that are desirable . . .

tantalizing. If a bhikkhu seeks delight in them . . . the Evil One can do with him as he wishes.[33]

Many meditation students have told me that food is a strong "bait" and that they want to pay more attention to recognize the "hook" that might be hidden behind the lure. One student commented,

> Yesterday as I walked past a bakery, I saw the most perfect looking cinnamon roll. Many images, feelings, and thoughts arose instantaneously. I immediately bit the hook and bought the roll. I pictured myself enjoying this cinnamon roll as a reward for working hard lately. I told myself I deserved it. I created a story about needing to try this cinnamon roll because I am a connoisseur of sorts, and I make it my mission to find the best cinnamon rolls in my city.
>
> The hook only made its way deeper. I devoured this thing of perfection and I wanted to shout from the rooftops and share my discovery with the world—this particular cinnamon roll was definitely the best! I continued thinking about it throughout the day until I remembered the simile of the fish biting the hook. I was so hooked! I had devoted a remarkable amount of time to thinking; I was feeding my attachment to this cinnamon roll. Why did I create such a grand story around a piece of food that was gone in a few minutes? I can see now that my focus narrows when it is seeking gratification. The cinnamon rolls seemed to be promising physical, emotional, and personal gratification. I saw an enormous investment in I-making and my-making bound up in this simple thing. When Shaila asked, 'Do you really want to cling to things that are constantly changing?' I realized how deeply I had bit on the hook. These dangers are embedded in many daily choices that I routinely make.

When our minds are clouded by delusion, they are likened to foolish fish; they grasp onto defilements and do not see the dangers in them. Sometimes our comprehension of the threat is weak, and the thoughts of craving overpower our good intentions. Sometimes we convince ourselves that if we were not indulging our desires, life would be too bleak to endure. But some fish are able to live to a ripe old age. These smart fish see the hook. Aware of the danger, they avoid biting down on it.

Through the exercises in previous chapters, you have discerned wholesome and unwholesome states of mind and seen that pleasure can arise in both kinds of states. A craving for strawberry-rhubarb pie and a self-absorbed romantic fantasy might feel pleasant, but be harmful. Thoughts of kindness and generosity might also feel pleasant, but be beneficial. This training requires that you diligently look past the seductive qualities of enjoyable perceptions to see if the "hook" of craving is lying in wait. Is there a danger lurking behind that mask of pleasure?

To see past impulsive desires and avoid being blinded by harmful forces of craving, you will need to be familiar with your personal tendencies. What kind of thoughts and perceptions are most tempting? Just as different baits and hooks catch different types of fish, different perceptions will tantalize different people.

This practice does not prescribe a rigid, puritanical restraint, laden with judgment. But each practitioner will need to recognize his or her vulnerabilities and determine when it is skillful to heighten vigilance. A bar of chocolate may pose no dangers of attachment to some people, but to others, it may create an unhealthy craving that can spiral down into depression and remorse.

IMPULSES THAT LEAD TO ACTIONS

What kinds of impulses or thoughts most often arise in your mind? Do those thoughts fuel harmful obsessions with sensual desire, hate, or delusion? Assess the risks involved in repeating your habitual patterns, and the consequences they might lead to if unhealthy thoughts were to be expressed in speech or acted upon.

Danger can manifest in the three kinds of action: bodily action, verbal action, and mental action. You might notice craving that arises as you walk past the donut box in the office, the feeling of cold superiority when you judge the style of your friend's new shirt, or impatient indignation when you wait in a slow line or get stuck in traffic. Notice the tone of your thoughts (mental action), and the inner cues that foretell that you are about to say (verbal action) or do (bodily action) something you might later regret. Pause and replace the thought with a more skillful one or steer yourself toward an action that you will later respect. If you harbor angry beliefs, notice how they affect the words you speak and the decisions you make. If you are attached to your political views, consider that this obstinance might prevent you from understanding how a situation affects others.

When you fully experience and recognize the price of repeating your unskillful habits—like *feeling* the burn from the hot stove rather than just *knowing* the stove is hot—those old patterns will not maintain their charm. While that familiar habit once seemed to bring happiness, you may now see that it actually leads to anguish. When you see this clearly, the attractiveness fades, the clinging ends, and you will find that it becomes easier to accomplish something both simple and powerful—focused attention on the task at hand. Whether that task involves a daily activity, a thought process, or the application of a meditation technique, connecting with present experience is a powerful alternative to the allure of habitual distractions.

By seeing the danger in certain kinds of thought patterns, you open the door to better options. If your aim is liberation, even the restless wandering mind is a dangerous state, because it obstructs concentration. A subtle tendency to entertain yourself with musical tunes running through the mind during meditation may not be evil, but this habit prevents clear seeing of what is happening now. Even innocuous mental chatter obstructs a continuity of mindfulness. Laziness is subtle, but alarming when our lack of energy allows other unwholesome states to fester. These mental states may not be as blatant as hate or jealously, but restlessness and laziness waste precious time, weaken wisdom, perpetuate agitation, feed hindrances, and delay spiritual development.

You have a limited amount of time in your life—do you want to fritter it away replaying trivial fantasies and miss this precious opportunity to develop the spiritual path? Informed by the dangers, you can make more skillful choices about what thoughts you will entertain and how you will work with the conditions of your mind.

A meditation student shared, "For me, it's popcorn. I have been watching what I eat in an attempt to lose weight. Friday evening I gave in and had a bowl of popcorn. Within twenty minutes of finishing that bowl of popcorn, I realized it wasn't worth the calories and I regretted doing it. I have stopped beating myself up so I didn't have too much remorse, but a careful examination of how I felt after eating revealed the craving that drove this activity. I was not even hungry."

He recognized that it was unproductive to beat himself up over this indulgence. Shaming or guilt-tripping himself would have only made him feel worse and might increase the desire for gratification. Instead, he reflected and came to a striking understanding—unrecognized craving drives many actions of body and mind.

A Delight beyond Sensual Pleasures

Sensual pleasures do not need to be obliterated, condemned, or feared, but a committed meditator will learn to meet them with mindfulness, know them with wisdom, contemplate their impermanence, recognize their limitations, and not be compelled by their

Examine the Danger. See the Hook!

For the next week, each day carefully examine the "danger" in an impulse or thought that arises in the course of your daily life. Reflect on the potential harm the thought could cause.

Ask yourself:

- ▶ If I continue to think in this way, where is it going to lead?
- ▶ What type of mental states will it condition for the future?
- ▶ Will it fuel thoughts that generate sensual desire, hate, or delusion?
- ▶ Do I want this pattern to become the inclination of my mind?

It can be surprising to realize how often thoughts sabotage our paths and lead us away from our nobler aims.

- ▶ What do anger, envy, and lust cost you or others?
- ▶ What effect do these unwholesome tendencies have on your relationships, your happiness, your health, your self-respect, and your meditative development?

Notice how habitual thoughts affect your worldly relationships and spiritual aspirations.

influence. Ignoring the impermanence of things inevitably leads to suffering when pleasant objects change or are no longer attainable. The Buddha explicitly taught that whoever seeks delight in the senses is seeking delight in suffering and therefore is not free from suffering.[34]

The Buddha was not always a renunciate. He was raised with the social comforts, sensual pleasures, and material luxuries available to a highborn noble of his time. He shared,

> Formerly when I lived the home life, I enjoyed myself, provided and endowed with the five cords of sensual pleasure: with forms cognizable by the eye ... with sounds cognizable by the ear ... with odours cognizable by the nose ... with flavours cognizable by the tongue ... with tangibles cognizable by the body that are wished for, desired, agreeable, and likable, connected with sensual desire, and provocative of lust. I had three palaces, one for the rainy season, one for the winter, and one for the summer. I lived in the rains palace for the four months of the rainy season, enjoying myself with musicians, none of whom were men, and I did not go down to the lower palace.
>
> On a later occasion, having understood as they actually are the origin, the disappearance, the gratification, the danger and the escape in the case of sensual pleasures, I abandoned craving for sensual pleasures, I removed fever for sensual pleasures, and I abided without thirst, with a mind inwardly at peace. I see other beings who are not free from lust for sensual pleasures being devoured by craving for sensual pleasures, burning with fever for sensual pleasures, indulging in sensual pleasure, and I do not envy them.[35]

You may worry that if you free your mind from the web of sensual pleasures your life will become intolerably bland. You might fear that you could lose the satisfaction of deep friendship, the inspiration for creative activities, the delight in watching a kitten play, the pride in creating a perfectly prepared custard, or the thrill of challenging your body to complete a marathon. This practice does not deny life's joys and triumphs, nor does it question your right to do what you enjoy doing. Importantly, it distinguishes between two incongruous outcomes: do your habits increase attachment to sensual pleasures, or do they support your spiritual growth?

Through meditation, one can access states of extraordinary pleasure and joy. When the mind is freed from distraction, unified, and concentrated, meditators can abide in deep absorptions called the *jhāna* states.

In the passage quoted above, the Buddha declared that he did not envy people who indulged in sensual pleasures. He made this declaration because he knew the greater pleasures, the sublime pleasures of concentration. In reference to the pleasure experienced during meditative absorption, he explained, "there is . . . a delight apart from sensual pleasures, apart from unwholesome states, which surpasses even divine bliss. Since I take delight in that, I do not envy what is inferior."[36]

Boldly look into your own mind and see whether seeking gratification in sensual pleasures is genuinely satisfying. I assure you that concentration is by far more blissful. Mindfulness, wisdom, meditation, and letting go are anything but dull. As your meditation practice deepens, you may experience for yourself the delight that cannot be found in sensual pleasures.

WHAT IS THE GRATIFICATION?

Pleasure isn't inherently a problem. It is quite possible to fully enjoy pleasant feelings without triggering craving and the exhausting pursuit of comfort. The practice of mindfulness enables us to be aware of pleasure without feeding cravings. Problems arise when we lose mindfulness, ignore impermanence, and become engrossed in the search for pleasant experiences. It is natural to enjoy pleasant encounters, but we must also be intelligent about what is developing in that moment of pleasure. A wise person learns to forgo short-term pleasures in favor of long-term happiness.

The Buddha taught:

> What is the gratification in the case of sensual pleasures? Bhikkhus, there are these five cords of sensual pleasure. What are the five? Forms cognizable by the eye that are wished for, desired, agreeable and likable, connected with sensual desire, and provocative of lust . . . sounds cognizable by the ear, odors cognizable by the nose, flavors cognizable by the tongue, tangibles cognizable by the body . . . Now the pleasure and joy that arise dependent on these five cords of sensual pleasure are the gratification in the case of sensual pleasures.[37]

Our preoccupation with thoughts of sensual desire can be heightened in times of uncertainty when there is no clear action to take or when we are emotionally upset. Even the slight discomfort that might arise in the transition between two projects might cause one to wander mindlessly toward the refrigerator or lure one into a daydream promising comfort or reward. The Buddha describes how an untrained person in pain will tend to reach for pleasure to counter the pain:

> Being contacted by painful feeling, he seeks delight in sensual pleasure. For what reason? Because the uninstructed worldling does not know of any escape from painful feeling other than sensual pleasure. When he seeks delight in sensual pleasure, the underlying tendency to lust for pleasant feeling lies behind this. He does not understand

as it really is the origin and the passing away, the gratification, the danger and the escape in the case of these
feelings.[38]

When you are able to meet pleasant feelings with mindfulness,
your attention will remain balanced and wisdom will grow. Try
this with your next bite of dessert, perhaps a spoonful of ice cream.
As you place a spoonful of this creamy, cold treat in your mouth,
endeavor to be fully present for the sensual delight of the sweet
flavor and soft texture as it melts on your tongue. Stay present
with the rich sensual experiences that occur during that one bite.
Enjoy it fully while it is present and watch it fade. Do not let craving anticipate the next bite while ice cream is still in your mouth.
Know pleasure when it is present, and also let it end. Learn to
be mindful of present pleasure, without allowing it to trigger the
defilement of craving.

Defilements only repeat when they have fuel; repetitive thoughts
are often fed by the anticipation of a reward. These thoughts can't
arise without supportive causes, and it is up to you to discover the
source of their nutriment. Contemplate whatever pleasure, benefit, or reward you believe you gain by thinking your distracting
thoughts.

Perhaps the assumed reward is as subtle as merely reinforcing an
identity, where you belong, or what you believe. It might strengthen
self-importance or create a feeling of comfort by giving you a sense
of control. Even a negative self-image can create a perverse sense of
security. Sometimes, even destructive patterns can seem oddly reas-
suring in their familiarity—that is also the gratification. Get familiar with the patterns that tantalize and lure you, and become aware
of the benefit you gain by allowing yourself to be seduced by them.

Mindfulness practices generally emphasize observing the affective quality of experience—that is, the feeling tone (*vedanā*).
This is the recognition of the pleasantness, unpleasantness, or

neither-pleasant-nor-unpleasant quality of any sensation, perception, or mental state.[39] When examining the reward you gain from habits, explore the pleasantness of that familiar rut. Look carefully—thoughts that reinforce a familiar sense of self might be providing a false sense of comfort.

Become mindful of pleasure as just a momentary experience of pleasure, without becoming trapped by it. When you rest in the awareness of a pleasant feeling without scheming to get more of it, you will notice that the feeling of pleasure arose due to conditions, and it will end when those conditions fade. By seeing *feeling* clearly, you will not struggle to try to make a pleasant experience last.

What Are the Dangers?

Material dangers and physical threats exist in the world, but the most frequent dangers that people encounter are the defilements connected with greed, anger, and delusion in their own minds.

The dangers in some thought patterns might be difficult to recognize; you might more easily identify the array of physical dangers and stressful conditions that certain thoughts initiate. Beginning with an initial desire for a sensual experience, a cascade of actions might ensue—bodily, verbal, and mental actions. You might struggle to acquire the experience that you desire; then struggle to maintain it, protect it, and increase your access to it.

Buddhist teachings compare one who seeks sensual pleasures to a man who is holding a blazing grass torch while walking against the wind. He gets burned, and as the teaching states, "[sensual pleasures] provide much suffering and much despair, while the danger in them is great."[40]

Many Dangers from Work to War

Most people work to support their needs. Amassing wealth merely to sustain sensual pleasures, however, can cause tremendous

⟶ *Highlighting Gratification*

Observe how the desire for reward functions in a variety of daily situations.

- ▶ How does it feel to experience gratification?
- ▶ How do you seek pleasure, benefits, rewards?
- ▶ Do you pursue gratification through food, sex, gifts, sights, relationships, controlling behaviors, fantasy, or by belonging to a social network?
- ▶ Do you seek gratification through intellectual or psychological pursuits, such as by seeking praise when you complete a task, reinforcing your identity through displays of knowledge, gaining social status by pleasing another person, or receiving benefits from fulfilling expected roles?
- ▶ What aspects of the meditation practice itself are gratifying for you?

Notice the many ways the desire for gratification manifests in your daily life. Notice whether, when you seek a reward, an attachment is strengthened.

suffering. In the Greater Discourse on the Mass of Suffering, the Buddha details many kinds of stress associated with the pursuit of sensory pleasure, which begin with learning a trade such as accounting, farming, husbandry, archery, or crafts and continue in establishing a business. If the business fails, one may suffer from that loss. If it succeeds, one must struggle to protect it from thieves, greedy heirs, and kings.[41]

People spend their hard-earned money to purchase things.

What is acquired must then be taken care of, maintained, repaired, guarded, insured, and then later disposed of. One might become upset if a cherished item is lost or broken.

Once wealth is acquired, one must manage that wealth. Conflicting opinions about how to spend, save, and use it could cause friction within marriages, arguments within families, and strife in communities. Disputes can expand beyond personal relations to clans, tribes, and states. Nations may form armies that "charge into battle massed in double array with arrows and spears flying and swords flashing," motivated largely by the pursuit or defense of possessions, pleasures, power, territory, or identities.[42] A great deal of suffering can develop out of the initial thought "I want."

The Buddhist discourses describe further problems: "Again with sensual pleasures as the cause . . . men break into houses, plunder wealth, commit burglary, ambush highways, seduce others' wives, and when caught," they will be punished. "With sensual pleasures as the cause, sensual pleasures as the source, sensual pleasures as the basis, the cause being simply sensual pleasures, people indulge in misconduct of body, speech and mind."[43] Prisons are filled with people who have been convicted of crimes motivated by greed.

Your pursuit of sensual pleasures may have less dramatic consequences. Do you ever take a second serving of food only to feel more bloated, uncomfortable, and self-critical later? Do you ever waste your time engaged in fantasy only to lose sleep and feel irritable the next morning? Have you ever returned home from a shopping mall with items that create more of a burden to take care of than the pleasure you gained from possessing them? Does your attempt to satisfy a particular desire exacerbate the tendency to cling to the thought "I want it" on future occasions? By not seeing the danger in the thought "I want," people proceed to behave in ways that produce painful conditions in the future.

Clinging to Things That Change

Attachment to even the most innocuous of pleasures spells danger—the frustration of trying to hold on to things that change. It is impossible to make that perfect moment last!

The Buddha recognized that sensual pleasures are impermanent. He taught, "that the eye . . . ear . . . nose . . . tongue . . . body . . . mind is impermanent, suffering, and subject to change: this is the danger in the eye . . . ear . . . nose . . . tongue . . . body . . . mind."[44] Every perception, possession, and encounter is impermanent, and therefore cannot be a reliable source of satisfaction—that is the ubiquitous danger.

I used to have a habit of enjoying a cup of tea in the late afternoon. During one long retreat my meditation teacher suggested that I renounce my tea break. Initially I rejected the suggestion, justifying that it was only tea, and not as strong as the coffee that others consumed. But my refusal to abandon my tea break highlighted a surprisingly strong attachment. So, reluctantly, I experimented with this modest act of renunciation. Once the decision was made, it was easy to forgo a cup of tea at 4:00 p.m.; after all, a cup of tea is a relatively simple thing to abandon.

Several days later, the tea urn that supplied us with hot water broke down. During the four days that it took to repair it, I watched other meditators approach the refreshment station with a cup in hand and depart with disappointment etched on their faces. The danger of expecting satisfaction through sensual pleasures, and the suffering that arises from that expectation, was evident. It was not just an afternoon cup of tea—that physical ritual was a reflection of thoughts that seemed to cry out, "I deserve a break. I need to have my way to be happy. I want this!" The absence of tea wasn't painful, but it became clear that habits of I-making and wanting produced discontent.

It is quite possible to appreciate an activity, an art form, a sensory encounter, or a skill without holding on to it. Relishing a bite of fresh watermelon, delighting in a horseback ride along forest trails, singing along to your favorite country-rock song, admiring sculptures in art galleries, solving intricate analytical problems, walking barefoot on damp grass, composing a well-articulated statement, enjoying the perfume of a rose in full bloom—these activities are not inherently damaging. However, indulging thoughts of desire for them, seeking gratification through attachment to them, and not recognizing their impermanence will inevitably lead to disappointment. Whether the attachment is embedded in the initial thoughts of wanting to have the experience, in the clinging to pleasures felt during the event, in the false sense of control that develops while planning for it, in the meaning produced by your internal commentary, or in the memories that you cling to afterward, there is stress.

We all engage in the world, enjoy pleasant tastes, touches, and sights, and perform a wide range of worldly activities. Indulging the desire for sensual pleasures was clearly prohibited for monastics. However, the Buddha recognized that sensual pleasures are part of a layperson's lifestyle. He taught that wealth that was rightly acquired could be enjoyed within the context of a lay lifestyle.[45] He did not expect all lay disciples to renounce every form of sensual pleasure and ordain as a renunciate. He said, "Householder, there are these four kinds of happiness that may be achieved by a lay person who enjoys sensual pleasures, depending on time and occasion. What four? The happiness of ownership, the happiness of enjoyment, the happiness of freedom from debt, and the happiness of blamelessness."[46] In this way, he encouraged lay practitioners to be guided by ethics, wisdom, and moderation in their activities.

A wise practitioner will remain alert for the distorting effects of lust, craving, and clinging amid sensory activities. These defilements tend to obscure the fact of change. By staying alert to the dangers of attachment, contemplating impermanence, and exposing thoughts of "I-want"-influenced behavior, adept practitioners learn to engage with pleasant activities without getting lost in them.

WHAT IS THE ESCAPE?

Abandoning the craving is the escape. It might come as soon as you clearly see the danger, or it might require an intentional nudge toward letting go. The Buddha taught "And, what is the escape in the case of sensual pleasures? It is the removal of desire and lust, the abandonment of desire and lust for sensual pleasures. This is the escape in the case of sensual pleasures."[47]

By seeing the danger, you gain a wise perspective that can remove the fuel for habitual cravings. Experiences remain pleasant and enjoyable, but the compelling aspect of craving fades away—sometimes immediately, sometimes more gradually.

For most people, habits do not vanish immediately and forever the first time we see the danger. An intellectual knowledge of the gratification, danger, and escape will not overcome the deeply conditioned urge to secure pleasurable rewards. To cultivate the escape route that the Buddha identifies, it is critical to interrupt the desire for gratification by pausing when you sense that your mind is lusting after an idea, craving for affirmation, enchanted by a thought, or greedily grasping for experience.

If initially the momentum of a habit is too strong and you are swept up by it, then simply watch your experience as the habit unfolds. Be curious and observe with care. Mindful observation will slow down the process and nourish a more spacious response, until eventually it becomes possible to choose to pause.

Then, gently put the brakes on the momentum of craving and wait for several minutes before taking any physical, verbal, or mental action toward the fulfillment of that desire.

Wait and watch your mind for ten or fifteen minutes. During that pause, support your potential to let go of the habitual pattern by physically moving away from the temptation (this is the next strategy, #3), by giving your mind a healthier alternative (replacing, strategy #1), or reflecting on the long-term reward of escaping from the bonds of that craving. Many distractions and habitual desires will simply fade away if you can wait and apply your mind skillfully for those minutes.

The Buddha taught a sensible, moderate, and balanced approach that he described as a middle way. It is not a path of austerity and discomfort, nor is it a journey of sensual indulgence. Disciples, even celibate monastics, are allowed to satisfy their need for food, clothing, shelter, medicines, and teachings. The Buddhist path advocates for a wise relationship to things, not a wholesale rejection of material comforts. The Buddha teaches:

> A bhikkhu is content with any kind of robe, and he speaks in praise of contentment with any kind of robe, and he does not engage in a wrong search, in what is improper, for the sake of a robe. If he does not get a robe he is not agitated, and if he gets one he uses it without being tied to it, infatuated with it, and blindly absorbed in it, seeing the danger in it, understanding the escape from it.[48]

These monastics do not reject material needs; they cultivate contentment with material things. Surely if a monastic can be content sleeping under a tree with no tent and accept whatever food or medicine is offered, we as lay people can abandon fussiness with our food, clothing, shelter, and medicine.

As laypeople we can develop contentment with our clothes, vehicles, houses, and myriad possessions. We address the problem of clinging and free the mind from the patterns that keep it attached to habitual distractions. Your examination of the danger of unwholesome thoughts and actions should not produce self-judgments. This reflective investigation requires self-inquiry, not self-condemnation. We are trying to understand our patterns, not prosecute ourselves for a perceived crime. Pursue your examination of dangers with a kind and curious attitude. Supported by a balanced and generous approach, this inquiry will weaken addictive attachments and lead to a cessation of those habitual impulses.

Now, aware of the danger of distraction, the healthier alternatives that you practiced in strategy #1 may seem even more important and appealing. Informed by this renewed awareness of the dangers that accompany defilements, your attempts to replace unwholesome thoughts with wholesome alternatives will become even more effective.

SEEING THE DANGER QUELLS SUFFERING

To quote the Buddha, "When one dwells contemplating danger in things that can be clung to, craving ceases. With the cessation of craving, comes the cessation of clinging; with the cessation of clinging, cessation of existence . . . cessation of birth . . . aging-and-death, sorrow, lamentation, pain, displeasure, and despair cease. Such is the cessation of this whole mass of suffering."[49]

He illustrates this with an image of a bonfire: when one does not cast dry grass, dry wood, dry cow dung, or other fuel on a bonfire, it gradually dies down. "Thus, when the former supply of fuel is exhausted, that great bonfire, not being fed with any more fuel, lacking sustenance, would be extinguished. So too, when one lives contemplating danger in things that can be clung to, craving ceases. . . . Such is the cessation of this whole mass of suffering."[50] If we remain aware of dangers, pleasant feelings come and go without becoming obstacles to our spiritual path.

Exposing the way thoughts may fuel or quench habitual patterns, we must bluntly ask ourselves: What has this habitual pattern or addictive urge done for me? And answer honestly. Perhaps it has caused you to overeat until your pants no longer fit comfortably, spend your way into debt, or just waste your time. Maybe you have let habitual desires and thoughts convince you to deceive colleagues, adopt beliefs that isolated you from family, or justify the betrayal of prior commitments. Note whether your thoughts are supporting or sabotaging your deepest aspirations. Are they nourishing your personal values and life goals or leaving you feeling ashamed?

This strategy of examining the dangers highlights the consequences of your actions. Whereas craving creates the illusion that gaining the object of desire is of vital importance, this strategy of examining the danger heightens the knowledge that habitual distractions offer only false promises. By evaluating the significance of habitual distractions, you shine a light on those thoughts, and they lose their importance. As their strength weakens, your everyday choices will become wiser. As you make skillful choices about what patterns you will reinforce, you will be able to give energy to your genuine priorities in life, and your actions will align with your noblest aims.

Summary of Main Points

You can defuse distracting thoughts by clearly identifying their harmful effects. The cycle of distracting thoughts tends to continue when there is an apparent reward. There can also be attachment to sensory pleasures, habitual actions, or the desire for personal approval. To practice the strategy of examining the danger, whenever you notice your mind lurching toward an object or experience, consider the consequences of pursuing that desire: the need to pay for and care for the object; the grief experienced when it is broken or lost; and the impact that this experience will have on family, community, and your spiritual development. Seeing the danger inclines the mind toward abandoning the sense of enchantment. When you remain aware of the danger, pleasant feelings can be enjoyed without clinging and can arise and dissipate without causing problems.

We have learned that thoughts are mental events that we can pay attention to. We've learned there are wholesome and unwholesome thoughts. We have practiced the first two strategies: (1) replacing

🍂 *Gratification, Danger, and Escape*

Choose a thought, pattern, or common reaction to examine. Analyze it by writing down how you understand its gratification, danger, and escape.

- ▸ What is the gratification?
- ▸ What do you get out of it?
- ▸ What is it serving?
- ▸ Is it fulfilling a craving for sense pleasure or personal need or confirming a view, value, or identity?
- ▸ What are the dangers?
- ▸ What are its costs? Risks?
- ▸ What is its impact on relationships? What do you give up (or lose) by nurturing this thought?
- ▸ Is it reliable or impermanent?
- ▸ Is it a cause of suffering or happiness?
- ▸ What is the escape in this situation?

Now look into some wise actions you could take:

- ▸ What are some alternative thoughts or reminders that might make a positive shift in the pattern?
- ▸ Could you starve the habit by working directly with the desire or fear that unwholesome thoughts feed on?
- ▸ What might be a healthier way of getting your genuine needs met?
- ▸ Does the change you seek require verbal or bodily action or a shift in the way you think?

detrimental thoughts with beneficial ones and (2) examining the danger in thoughts. As we recognize the deleterious effects that repeated unwholesome thoughts have on our behaviors, relationships, and emotional tendencies, we create opportunities to change our habits. As we adjust our manner of thinking and acting, restless thoughts will lose their potency. As our meditative skill develops, thoughts settle, and mindfulness and concentration come to the fore to support progress on the spiritual path.

CHAPTER 5

WITHDRAWING THE FUEL

Strategy #3—Avoid It, Ignore It, Forget It

When the mind is not obsessed, tireless energy is aroused, unmuddled mindfulness is set up, the body becomes tranquil and untroubled, the mind becomes concentrated and one-pointed.
—CONNECTED DISCOURSES OF THE BUDDHA[51]

WE NURTURE WISE ATTENTION by distinguishing beneficial thoughts from harmful ones. Wise attention optimizes each moment to incline the mind toward skillful states such as those that promote concentration and insight. In chapter 3 you developed the skill of replacing unwholesome thoughts with wholesome ones. Then, in chapter 4, you learned to reflect on the dangers in unwholesome thoughts to help you determine what to pursue and what to avoid. If these exercises have not yet removed the distraction, you can try the next strategy—ignore it, avoid it, forget it, turn your attention away from it.

With this sequence of strategies in mind, you hold a detailed road map for developing attention. The Buddha articulates this way of developing wise discernment: "There are two kinds of happiness: the kind to be pursued and the kind to be avoided. When I observed that in the pursuit of such happiness, unwholesome factors increased and wholesome factors decreased, then that happiness was to be avoided. And when I observed that in the pursuit of such happiness unwholesome factors decreased and wholesome ones increased, then that happiness was to be sought after."[52]

In this chapter we will consider the advice to "try to forget those thoughts, and not give attention to them."[53] An earnest meditation student might argue that ignoring experience sounds like the opposite of mindfulness practice. After all, aren't we supposed to be open, allowing, and receptive to the full gamut of our experience? There may be situations, however, when ignoring could be the most skillful response.

Imagine you want to lose a few pounds and you start a diet. The next day, you enter your workplace for a staff meeting to discover a large platter of pastries. Would it be wise to sit down right in front of the pastries, fixate on them, and drool with desire? Does it help to lash out in anger at the colleague who provided the snacks? If seeing the platter of pastries triggers craving, anger, or self-loathing, give yourself a break from the painful trigger of staring at baked goods. Take a seat further away. You can simply turn attention away from habitual triggers, withdraw your interest, and let your attention dwell somewhere else with perceptions that support your goals.

WISDOM OF SEEING AND NOT-SEEING

The Buddha compares the strategy of ignoring to people with good eyesight who can easily open and close their eyes. Similarly, we have the option to engage with sensory and mental phenomena—or not. We can either give time and energy to a perception or thought pattern or withdraw our attention from it.

Habitual thought patterns can be triggered by the environments we find ourselves in. For example, walking past a bar might stimulate the desire for a drink, watching a movie might seem to require popcorn to complete the experience, feeling annoyed might trigger the urge to self-soothe with a cookie, receiving criticism might trigger self-deprecating or blaming thoughts. Habitual thoughts and urges are hard to ignore because they are reinforced by emotions and intertwined with a sense of personal identity.

Given all this, this teaching might sound simplistic, unrealistic, and perhaps unwise: "If you don't want to see something, don't look at it, and if you don't want to think something, don't think about it!" If it were easy to forget obsessive thoughts, they wouldn't be obsessive. If all our problems could be resolved by ignoring them, we would surely be living in a more ethical world. Nevertheless, it can be empowering to consider the possibility of simply turning away in some situations. This instruction could be one step toward expanding your options.

Research shows that we can successfully ignore much more sensory stimuli than we think we can. Psychological research has repeatedly demonstrated that attention is selective. We are constantly bombarded with sensory input from the five sense doors; a single square centimeter of an olfactory sense organ can contain millions of sensory neurons. In addition, the mind door processes uncountable mental impressions of images, memories, and thoughts. Our minds must constantly filter which sensations are worthy of being brought to our conscious attention and which can be ignored.[54]

In a famous study at Harvard University, researchers tested the limits of attention by asking student volunteers to watch a short video of two teams passing around a basketball. The students were instructed to count the number of times the basketball got passed between players.[55] As they intently watched and counted basketball passes, a woman wearing a gorilla suit strolled into the action on the court. The gorilla faced the camera, thumped its chest, and then left the court. Half of the students reported not having seen the gorilla. In repeated experiments in various countries, the results were the same.

The volunteers were attentive and watchful, but they were so engrossed in their task, primed to look for basketball passes, that extraneous information was completely ignored. Some participants in this study who were shown the video replay of the experiment could not believe it was the same video they initially saw and insisted there had never been someone in a gorilla suit on the court.

Information that is superfluous to our focus or does not fit with our prescribed assumptions is much less likely to make an impression on consciousness. We tend to perceive what we expect to and want to perceive, and when we are paying attention to one thing, we might be ignoring something else.

Selective attention can cause us to look at the world incorrectly because we tend to see only what we already believe and ignore observations that do not fit into our model of the world. For example, depressed individuals might remember only tragic events in their lives and forget their happy memories. Those who have low self-esteem might frequently think about their failures and ignore their past successes. People who suffer from anxiety attacks might dwell on traumatic events and be oblivious to the routine and potentially joyful events that occur every day. If romantic relationships end in betrayal, lovers might focus on the undesirable qualities of their partners and forget why they fell in love in the first place. Polarized thinking of this kind prevents people from seeing the world as it really is. It can even shift a beautiful or neutral perception into something scary and threatening.

Another example of the limited capacity of our attention can be found in traffic laws that prohibit texting or using a phone while driving. When attention is occupied with a conversation, less cognitive bandwidth is available to process traffic conditions. Even hands-free systems have been shown to restrict the range of attention and create a kind of tunnel vision, focusing attention only on the lane in front and eliminating peripheral vision. By giving attention to one thing, we are not noticing something else. Even if we follow safe driving habits, we might still occasionally miss our freeway exit when we are engaged in heated imaginary conversations in our own minds.

These studies show that we already have the ability to ignore a lot! What can we do to refine our natural aptitude for selective attention so that we can direct our attention more skillfully? It might help to broaden the field of attention, expand our perspectives, and notice more that is happening around us. At other times, it might be better to narrow the scope of attention to steer clear of harmful patterns. By learning to be more aware of what our mind is focused on and what is excluded from its attention, we can enhance mindfulness and steer our engagement toward greater well-being.

ERASING UNWANTED TENDENCIES

Training attention to consistently support our spiritual path means that we must stop habitually following conditioned patterns of distraction. Mindfulness shows us that there are pathways we don't want to go down. When they arise in the mind, we have the option of not following them.

While others might amuse themselves with fantasy, make selfish decisions, and indulge in worry and fretting, you are not compelled to do the same. By understanding how the human mind works and observing your own mind, you can develop the tools to skillfully manage your thought habits. Just as the pilot of a ship slowly turns the wheel to change its direction, through practice you can steer your mind away from danger.

A discourse called Effacement in the *Middle Length Discourses of the Buddha* enumerates a list of forty-four harmful qualities and actions; their absence is described as the antidote to their presence. The title of this discourse highlights the term *effacement*, which means "to erase, make disappear, withdraw." In this teaching on forty-four ways of making defilements disappear, the Buddha reminds his disciples that "even the inclination of mind toward wholesome states is of great benefit" and even greater benefit comes through dedicated bodily and verbal actions.[56]

The Buddha taught:

> Others will be cruel; we shall not be cruel here: effacement should be practiced thus.
>
> Others will kill living beings; we shall abstain from killing living beings here: effacement should be practiced thus. . . .
>
> Others will speak falsehood; we shall abstain from false speech here: effacement should be practiced thus.
>
> Others will gossip . . .
>
> Others will be envious . . .
>
> Others will be deceitful . . .
>
> Others will be arrogant . . .
>
> Others will be difficult to admonish . . .
>
> Others will be lazy . . .
>
> Others will be unmindful . . .
>
> Others will adhere to their own views, hold on to them tenaciously, and relinquish them with difficulty; we shall not adhere to our own views or hold on to them tenaciously, but shall relinquish them easily: effacement should be practiced thus.[57]

The discourse lists a total of forty-four such defilements presented in this structure.

A Powerful Pause

The discourse on Effacement repeats the same list of forty-four defilements in light of personal tendencies. The Buddha suggests, "A person given to killing living beings has abstention from killing living beings by which to avoid it . . . One given to gossip has abstention from gossip by which to avoid it . . . One given to restlessness has non-restlessness by which to avoid it . . . One given to fraud has non-fraud by which to avoid it . . . One given to negligence has diligence by which to avoid it . . . One given to laziness has the arousal of energy by which to avoid it . . ."[58]

Many unwanted habitual patterns can be countered by simply stopping. If you can pause before unleashing habitual unwholesome chain reactions, you might discover that stopping becomes a remarkably viable alternative. In the moment of that pause, you are observing rather than reacting to experience.

Pausing makes it possible to perceive and choose a radically different path. The Buddha reminds us that there are options to our habits: "Suppose there were an uneven path and another even path by which to avoid it . . ."[59] Just as a traveler with the wish to complete their journey safely would not choose an uneven path if an even path were available, a wise person would opt for the more skillful option even if it were less familiar.

Habits have become habits because we have repeatedly nourished them with energy, time, and attention. In the language of contemporary neuroscience, our brains are continually creating neural highways and reinforcing tendencies through repetitive actions. The synapse connectivity of the neural pathways we use most frequently will strengthen. But even if we find ourselves caught in a deep rut, a brief pause can be powerful. It can prepare the mind to choose a nonhabituated route. We might opt for the even path that the Buddha describes, a path that leads to happiness, freedom, and peace.

Even if our habits are easily triggered, and we often indulge in them, and their momentum feels strong, we are not compelled to go with the habitual flow of energy. We can stop. But to successfully discontinue those thoughts, we will need the support of concentration and clear intention.

How Do You Use Your Mind?

The key to this strategy of ignoring, avoiding, forgetting is developing the skill to withdraw your attention from mental entanglements, thereby realizing that you can choose how you use your mind. It appears similar to strategy #1 (replacing), but with less emphasis on what you turn your attention toward and more focus on your capacity to pull your energy away from the magnetic force of habit. For example, when you let go of an angry thought and shift to thoughts of loving-kindness, strategy #1 manifests in the replacing of anger with benevolence, and strategy #3 is demonstrated by the withdrawal of attention from the triggers that feed anger. By training to withdraw attention, you strengthen your capacity for restraint.

Strategy #3 teaches you to leverage the innate human ability to select where you put your attention. Instead of reinforcing habitual biases that obscure unexpected perceptions, you are cultivating the skill to restrain and guide your attention wisely. You learn to consciously restrict the field of attention to those perceptions you deem helpful. You refuse to be pulled into the seductive vortex of familiar fantasies, personal dramas, and chronic worries. You learn not to think the thoughts that you do not want to think. When a mental pattern no longer captures your attention, it eventually subsides and withers away from lack of fuel.

One meditation student did not understand the value of this strategy until the day her partner lashed out in a verbal tirade over some perceived offense. As she withdrew her attention from the harsh words, she turned her mind to observe how her reactions manifested in her body.

She was mindful that defensive thoughts were arising: "It wasn't my fault! You're misinterpreting my intentions! This problem is yours, not mine!" Instead of verbalizing her reactive thoughts, she immediately chose to abandon them. She silently recited a phrase

---

Billable Hours

Whenever you find unproductive, repetitive thoughts dominating your mind, you can find creative and effective ways to stop thinking them.

Choose a mental habit you want to change and apply billable hours to it. Each time you find yourself ruminating, worrying, or thinking the thoughts that you decided to put out of your mind, pay for the time you spent dwelling on them. Set a rate that is compatible with your hourly wages and pay according to the amount of time you spent thinking those thoughts. For example, if you spent two minutes worrying and you make $60 per hour, put $2 in a special container and give the money to charity.

Eventually, as your skill in directing your attention increases, you'll have the flexibility to turn your attention toward or away from thoughts and perceptions at will.

This will enable you to relax when it is time to relax, observe when it is appropriate to observe, reflect when it is useful to reflect, and move confidently into action when it is the right time to act.

that inspired her. "Abandoning reactivity requires the utmost courage." Instead of responding with her typical defensive pattern, she redirected her attention to her bodily sensations—tightness and constriction in her belly, chest, and throat—recognizing them as strong and uncomfortable, but bearable and not dangerous. Finally, she reminded herself of the peaceful spaciousness that is available once reactive thoughts are abandoned. The physical, emotional, and interpersonal tensions soon diminished, supporting calmer and clearer communication.

The more she practiced this way, the more vividly she recognized that it was an illusion to think that her defensive reactivity would provide the self-protection and self-nourishment that she desired. Over time, she experienced a sense of peaceful spaciousness and profound equanimity with increasing frequency. It's a virtuous cycle that makes it easier and easier to abandon thoughts and the reactivity associated with them. By not reacting defensively in the moment, she gives herself and her partner time to calm down, see each other's perspective, and try to reconcile.

PICK YOUR BATTLES

Ambitious meditators can sometimes push themselves more quickly than their meditative skill warrants. They might explore a defilement so vigorously that they feel overwhelmed and want to quit.

If you are compelled to confront every situation, you will likely exhaust your energy and lose touch with your priorities. Sometimes it is better to ignore an event, preserve your energy, and practice serenity or cultivate concentration. To progress on this path, you will need the flexibility to confront a thought process head-on, but also to cautiously back off when warranted.

There are probably times when the sound of a phone ringing interrupts your focus. You might be in the middle of a phone conversation and be distracted by the call-waiting signals in the background on your device. Often it is best to abandon the curiosity to see who called and just ignore the notification tone.

A student told me that she enjoyed a weekly yoga class, but often felt irritated by the cacophony of ringtones coming from the coat and shoe area. When the sounds seemed to interrupt her experience of serenity, she reminded herself not to let innocuous sounds trigger the defilements.

We can pick our battles skillfully and choose to ignore some experiences. When you intuit that any level of engagement will likely fuel a hindrance such as desire or aversion, practice this strategy of avoiding, ignoring, and forgetting.

Avoid

A careful and wise person avoids apparent dangers: a recovering alcoholic might wisely avoid hanging out in bars, a person with anxiety might limit the number of news broadcasts she listens to each day, and a sensible nurse would wear a protective facemask before helping a contagious patient.

The Buddha said that one

> reflecting wisely, avoids a wild elephant, a wild horse, a wild bull, a wild dog, a snake, a stump, a bramble patch, a chasm, a cliff, a cesspit, a sewer. Reflecting wisely, one avoids sitting on unsuitable seats, wandering to unsuitable resorts, and associating with bad friends, since if one were to do so, wise companions in the holy life might suspect one of evil conduct. While taints, vexation, and fever might arise in one who does not avoid these things, there are no taints, vexation, and fever in one who avoids them. These are the taints that should be abandoned by avoiding.[60]

When you know the danger (that is, when you see the hook), your instinct for self-preservation will kick in and quickly move you away from the threat.

The Buddha did not suggest that his disciples avoid all difficult situations. You cannot avoid all pain, illness, unwanted changes, or death. You cannot control other people or eliminate all unjust conditions in the world. You probably did not choose your family members, office mates, or the politicians that govern your community. Some situations are unavoidable.

There are, however, some situations for which a skillful withdrawal might be a strategic option. When you are surfing and see a great white shark swimming nearby, it might be a good idea to get out of the water for a while. When you see your colleagues gossiping about the boss in the pantry area, you can turn the corner and walk away from them. Similarly, when you know that nothing good will come from indulging a habitual train of thought, it is a good idea to give it a wide berth.

IGNORE

When my family adopted a nine-year-old calico cat from the local shelter, the whole household went through a period of adjustment. She was a good-natured cat, but exploring her new home and family involved figuring out her boundaries and determining what we would and would not tolerate: how far could she push to get what she wanted?

She tried various catlike maneuvers. The most unpleasant was waking us up in the morning by hitting our sleeping faces with her paw. The first tap was gentle, but if we didn't wake up, she began pounding more aggressively and putting out her claws. Since her basic needs for food, playtime, grooming, sunbathing, and a clean litter box were routinely satisfied, we believed that she just wanted attention. Our strategy was basically to ignore her when she beat on us, and mostly it worked. Only rarely did we need to employ stronger expressions of disapproval before she quit this predawn punching game.

While you might sometimes find that your unruly defilements are pestering you, you do not always need to engage with them—they might gradually subside just by not being fueled. Do not deny that they are present; simply refuse to feed defilements by flattering them with your attention.

Whatever your usual obsessions might be, try to set some reasonable limits. For example, you might practice dealing with work issues at work, but not bringing them into your home. In order to fall asleep at night, you must temporarily stop fretting over your concerns and allow the mind to rest. Write down your priorities for tomorrow and trust that you will deal with your troubles then, at an appropriate time.

Participants at meditation retreats perform simple daily kitchen and housekeeping chores that allow them to practice being intentionally present with what they are doing: not thinking about making salad while sitting in the meditation hall and not wishing to be sitting in the meditation hall while washing dishes. You can train yourself to be present in this way and thereby put aside potentially intrusive thoughts.

Not My Business!

One of my students could see her faultfinding and self-critical thoughts clearly. She could recognize an inner tirade directed at people she saw in her neighborhood, on TV, or in her family. "You are not doing it right! It should be done like this! How could you act that way? You idiot!"

Wherever she looked, she saw what was "wrong" and scurried about trying to fix everything. When walking out of a restaurant, she felt compelled to straighten the chairs others left askew while mentally castigating their laziness. Strolling along the main street downtown, she would hate the people that she imagined had left litter on the street, and then become so preoccupied with picking up trash that she forgot the errand that brought her downtown in the first place. While everyone knows it is good manners to push in your chair when you get up from a table, and it is one's civic duty to avoid littering, she felt deeply disturbed when her attention was so painfully hijacked by these behaviors. She did not feel joy when picking up trash, as others might with an act of generosity. Affected by her hypercritical judgments, she lived an angry, irritated existence.

Recognizing this painful hypercritical tendency, she worked diligently to observe and overcome it. When she noticed the pattern occurring, she would remind herself with a gentle, clear inner voice, "Not my business. Not my responsibility. I can't control the world." Repeated dozens of times a day, these little reminders have transformed her interactions and given her the flexibility to sometimes help and sometimes just step back and ignore the disturbing perception.

There is no end to the faults found by a mind inclined toward criticism and blame. If allowed to run rampant, chronic judging and faultfinding could occupy a lifetime, leaving little room for constructive development. Sometimes it is better to walk away and ignore it. Perhaps we will return later, when conditions ripen, and address the situation effectively. Or maybe we will just move on with our lives and forget about it.

FORGET

Do you spend your meditation sessions rehashing memories that trigger anger or fear? Do you take worries to bed with you in your thoughts and dreams? Resentment, worry, regrets, and fears are reinforced by thoughts—they can build into crippling anxiety or harsh grudges. These are the kinds of thoughts that might be better forgotten.

🐚 *Not My Business!*

Setting boundaries around thoughts can be especially help-ful for people who describe themselves as chronic fixers, habitual faultfinders, or possessing strong aversive or con-trolling tendencies. If you identify with one of these pat-terns, develop some phrases to remind yourself that you do not need to intervene in every situation.

For example, you might remind yourself:

- ► This is not my business.
- ► It is just an opinion.
- ► I'm not a mind reader; I don't know everything.
- ► I can't predict the future.
- ► Let's see how it develops.
- ► I can't control the world.
- ► Not my problem.
- ► This is how it is.

Then, whenever a judging or controlling thought arises, remind yourself to relax by reciting your phrase of good counsel.

This exercise should not prevent you from caring about the state of the world and taking action. Not all problems should be ignored. But you can develop enough flexibility that when you do engage you do so consciously and wisely rather than manifesting familiar compulsive and control-ling habits.

Consider whether reminding yourself of the many ways you were wronged brings you closer to resolution or fans the flames of your outrage. To subdue grudges and dispel resentment, the Buddha recommended five approaches. One of these was to forget, disregard, or pay no attention to the person that you resent. He taught, "one should disregard the person one resents and pay no attention to him; in this way one should remove the resentment toward that person."[61]

Emotional healing requires the ability to let go of the past. Whether the harm was caused by the actions of another or by your own foolishness, you can stop dwelling on thoughts that strengthen anger or trigger fear and shame. This kind of ignoring does not deny the pain associated with those events. But if you find that dwelling on toxic worries, traumatic memories, or thoughts of your vulnerability magnifies suffering, give yourself the opportunity to not keep those experiences vividly alive in your mind.

If you find you are tormenting yourself by remembering your most embarrassing moments, do yourself a kind favor and just forget it happened. Set aside those thoughts, perhaps just for a while, now and then. Everyone does foolish and embarrassing things; everyone experiences failures in life. No one consistently presents their best qualities to the world. We must learn to sometimes shrug off our losses, dismiss our mistakes, and forget our shameful moments so we are available to be present now.

Healing from trauma is a gradual process, requiring sensitivity and patience. It can include skillfully revisiting the past to enhance your understanding and accept your feelings. It can also involve improving your connection with present lived experience. You might need to give yourself permission to stop allowing painful memories to occupy space in your mind. Learn to dispel them; trust that you can grow past them.

When you recognize that relentless repetition of those thoughts causes harm, give yourself the option to leave them behind. Moving forward in your life does not deny your pain; it does not acquiesce to injustice, and it is not an absolution of past crimes. You will feel what you feel, and you will learn through the experiences in your life. As you refine your skills in working mindfully with thoughts, you will be able to determine which thoughts, interpretations, and memories to foster and nourish. This ability to guide your attention away from harmful thoughts is key to developing resilience in the face of trauma.

People respond very differently to traumatic events—some recover quickly while others can experience debilitating symptoms that persist for years. Contemporary researchers are working to identify the factors that increase one's risk for prolonged posttraumatic responses and to propose methods that can build resilience to potentially stressful events.

A study of the aftermath of the Boston Marathon bombing by researchers at the University of California at Irvine found several predictors of acute stress symptoms: (1) being present at the bombing or knowing someone who was directly affected, (2) previous exposure to traumatic events such as the 9/11 terrorist attacks, (3) a history of mental illness, and (4) having watched six or more hours each day of media coverage in the aftermath of the event. This fourth factor turned out to be highly predictive of high-stress reactions.[62]

This may not be a surprise to readers—you have probably already recognized that repeated exposure, whether through external media or internal rumination, perpetuates stress. Many other psychological studies have found correlations between the tendency toward rumination and the prolonged experience of depression and post-traumatic stress symptoms.[63]

Thus, evidence supports the suggestion that it can be beneficial to skillfully withdraw the mental energy that feeds harmful thoughts. Through the practice of meditation, you can train yourself to stop giving your habitual defilements any more of your time.

You may not be ready or willing right now to completely forgive yourself, to understand the people who harmed you, or to love the world at large, but every bit of letting go supports the heart's healing from past shame and trauma. Sometimes experiences that cause acute pain or shame are the very ones that will fortify your commitment to sobriety, honesty, spiritual development, and an unshakable commitment to act with virtue in the future.

You may need to reflect on the painful memory or shameful action to gain a fuller understanding before you move past it. Then, when you are ready, you can give yourself permission not to dwell upon painful thoughts. Focus on your growth, strength, and virtue instead.

DISTRACT

Sometimes a little skillful distraction is the most effective method for taking the mind off disturbing thoughts. Have you developed an effective way to take a break from persistent obsessions in your ordinary activities? When caught in worldly worries, you might call a friend and talk about a sports event. Reading a novel, dancing to your favorite music, playing tennis, knitting on the porch, hopping on your exercise bike, or stepping outside to gaze at the starry sky can temporarily give the mind a much-needed break.

Compassionate acts of service might be even more powerful than worldly hobbies. A friend told me that when he felt depressed, he would go out and help someone. He might help an elderly neighbor trim the bushes, divide a watermelon into quarters and share the wedges with neighbors who live alone, stop by the nursing home to visit a friend, or volunteer at the local soup kitchen. Compassionate actions like these can improve our moods and free our minds from current obsessions.

A strategic distraction can remove unwholesome thoughts and focus attention on what is most useful. Such distractions create a much-needed pause in the habitual pattern and can give your mind the chance to relax, unwind, let go, and reset. Just a few minutes of an alternative activity might be an effective intervention to free the mind from habitual ruts.

Although the suggestions here might seem to overlap considerably with the strategy of replacing that was covered in chapter 3, the emphasis here is on your ability to withdraw the interest and pull away; the perception that is substituted is secondary.

Even when conditions are agreeable, meditation does not always go smoothly. In one teaching the Buddha suggests that if, while practicing mindfulness, one finds oneself overcome by sluggishness, anger, or distraction, "that bhikkhu should then direct his mind toward some inspiring sign. When he directs his mind toward some inspiring sign, gladness is born. When he is gladdened, rapture is born. When the mind is uplifted by rapture, the body becomes tranquil. One tranquil in body experiences happiness. The mind of one who is happy becomes concentrated. He reflects thus: 'The purpose for the sake of which I directed my mind has been achieved. Let me now withdraw it.'"[64]

Even if you have sat down with the intention to work with one meditation subject, there are times when it is wise to take a break from your primary practice and refresh your meditative attention with an "inspiring sign." You might do some loving-kindness practice, contemplate death, reflect on the qualities of the Buddha, investigate feelings, analyze a sensory perception, or shift attention to a different sense door. You are not forced to stay riveted to one meditative perception—you can skillfully adjust your practice to maintain a balanced, joyful interest in the development of your mind.

There are appropriate times for distraction. A parent might dangle a set of keys or a toy rattle in front of a crying baby—the screaming stops and she smiles. The child's attention is no longer obsessed with whatever caused her to scream; now she is fascinated by the dangling keys. When your mind is having a tantrum, dangle something else in front of your attention to help recompose and soothe yourself. Use the shift in perception to ground your attention in the present, remembering, "Oh, this is what's happening now."

Traditional suggestions for skillful distractions include reflecting on noble qualities of the Buddha or your teacher, or chanting Dhamma verses. Reciting a verse of wisdom can shift the mind toward wholesome thoughts.

If reflections and recitations fail to settle your mind, you might do some simple chores and focus your attention on what you are presently doing. The ancient commentaries suggest that a monk inventory his possessions.[65] The monk is told to go to his bag and take out each of the items, identifying them one by one: "This is a toothbrush. This is a spoon. This is a sewing kit. This is a nail-cutter." I compare this to housecleaning. When I felt upset as a teenager, I would gather my wits by cleaning a drawer, organizing my desk, or filing papers—simple, unexciting activities.

Meditators should select their distractions carefully. You should be able to easily return attention to your primary meditation practice (or the activity at hand). Choose wholesome or neutral activities that engage and organize attention but do not stimulate exuberant excitement or create an internal drama that feeds sensual desire, aversion, comparison, or fear. A distraction should produce calmness and ease, not increase your workload or exacerbate your worry. It should help you compose yourself and refresh your energy but not keep you awake at night developing an exciting new project.

During long, silent retreats, it is almost inevitable that enthusiasm will not remain high every moment of every day. Acceptable distractions can refresh your energy and provide a break. Inspired by the innocuous and almost dull character of the commentarial recommendations, I have developed a personal list of allowable distractions on retreats, including cleaning my room, doing laundry, taking a walk, mending clothes, flossing my teeth, and volunteering for an extra housekeeping chore. These activities give me something to do when I do not want to meditate, but they are not exciting enough to stimulate additional disruptive thoughts. And as a bonus I often feel slightly virtuous after I floss my teeth or darn my socks. The tasks can be performed mindfully, and then I get back to my meditation practice.

A meditation retreat is not the appropriate time for exciting activities. It is not the time to write a new book, begin a new project, or get caught up on the wide range of productive worldly activities that usually fill to-do lists. If your mind is agitated and you feel you just can't keep facing the same thoughts, get your needle and thread and sew up holes in your socks. Don't design a pattern for a whole new outfit; only do enough to take your mind off the obsession.

TAKE A BREAK

Avoidance should not become your primary approach to spiritual development. Mindfully and directly meeting the full array of feelings, perceptions, and experiences is generally a more effective approach to personal, social, and spiritual transformation. There are times, however, when you may not have the capacity to deal wisely with what is happening.

If your body and mind are excessively reactive, it might be better to take a break: soak in pleasure by letting the sun warm your back, smile as you watch squirrels playing in the trees, feel the soft suds of soap as you wash the dishes, delight in the distinctive scent of autumn as you rake leaves in your yard, or enjoy refining your golf swing. Ordinary pleasures can reset your stress response and reduce agitation.

This take-a-break approach should not create a habit of seeking pleasure to soothe or avoid emotional discomfort. For example, compulsive snacking is not a healthy long-term strategy for calming the mind. Nevertheless, intentionally relishing ordinary pleasures can sometimes knock the mind out of its negative cycles and restore

ᜩ *Skillful Distractions*

We all need to distract ourselves from our own thoughts at times, but is the distraction you have chosen a skillful one? Does it refresh your attention, restore your confidence, and lead you toward your goal?

Develop a list of skillful distractions to employ when you feel agitated by your thoughts.

For example, to distract yourself from obsessive thoughts in daily life you might:

- ▸ Organize a desk drawer
- ▸ Sort your mail
- ▸ Mend clothes
- ▸ Weed the flower bed
- ▸ Solve a crossword puzzle
- ▸ Invite friends over to play Scrabble
- ▸ Step outside
- ▸ Exercise or stretch
- ▸ Listen to soothing music or perhaps stimulating music that moves you to dance
- ▸ Call an old friend
- ▸ Try a new soup recipe

To distract yourself from obsessive thought in meditation you might:

> ▸ Count the breaths
> ▸ Change the object of attention for a few minutes, for example, by listening to sounds
> ▸ Move attention through a sequence of touchpoints
> ▸ Recite the refuges and precepts
> ▸ Contemplate your virtues or good qualities
> ▸ Visualize an inspiring image—perhaps a Buddha image
> ▸ Reflect on your intention
> ▸ Memorize and recite a Dhamma verse

your balance. Mindfully experiencing wholesome joy can brighten and inspire the mind. You can find a suitable time later to deal with the personal, psychological, social, or practical issues that need your attention.

There are times when you might need to give yourself a break by stepping back from the conditions that trigger reactions. After having distanced yourself from the habitual turmoil, you might find that you are quite capable of and interested in exploring your thought habits with mindful investigation (this inquiry is the topic of the next chapter). You might also need a more extended break to build up internal strength and supportive conditions.

Imagine that you can place your habitual thoughts in a drawer to await the time when you are ready to be mindful of them. Later you can pull them out, but for now they are out of sight and not actively demanding your attention. In the future you might bring a fresh perspective to the issues behind these thoughts, but for now you prefer to focus on developing inner resources that will make it possible to address the issues skillfully.

Ignoring is not quitting, but taking a graceful pause. When electronic devices malfunction, unplugging or shutting them down, waiting a few minutes, and then restarting can work wonders. Often a reboot is just the right cure for a troubled device. Not all your issues need to be unpacked in detail; not all unwholesome patterns need to be thoroughly examined. It is possible that you might just grow past your problems and find that the habits stop arising without requiring further attention. The significance of your stories might fade away and be forgotten with time as you move on with the next events of your life.

WHEN CONDITIONS ARE NOT RIPE

One student found herself forcefully trying to ignore distracting thoughts. She was eager to quickly forget her habitual distractions, but her efforts soon deteriorated into a tense desire to get rid of unpleasant conditions. Because she had neither developed skillful alternatives nor fully recognized the danger (strategies #1 and #2), this withdrawal of attention was not very helpful without the support of the preliminary strategies, so she changed her approach and took just a modest step back from the momentum of habitual thoughts to pause, feel present sensations in the body, and reflect on the pattern. In this way she found the ability to gently set healthier boundaries for her thoughts.

There are times when a direct approach is ill-advised and likely to be unsuccessful. At one time a monk named Venerable Meghiya was serving as the Buddha's attendant. Meghiya found a tranquil grove near a delightful stream and felt inspired to go there to practice meditation in seclusion. Aware that Meghiya was not yet mature enough to benefit from the intensity of solitary meditation, the Buddha tried to discourage him from meditating alone in the forest. Blinded by his own conceit, Meghiya departed against the Buddha's advice. Sure enough, he was overwhelmed by hindrances and soon returned to the company of the Buddha.

The Buddha explained that when the development of one's mind is immature, one should cultivate five conditions that incline toward maturity. One should (1) cultivate good friendships, (2) develop virtue, (3) discuss the Dhamma, (4) apply wise effort, and (5) possess a penetrative understanding of the arising and disappearance of phenomena.[66]

We must be realistic in our assessment of our meditative skills. Take the time to lay a strong foundation for your practice. Do not assume that you should be able to accomplish something just because you want it. Overconfidence is not conviction; it may be the deluded effects of conceit, arrogance, and misperception. Consider whether you have cultivated the skills and obtained the conditions that will support your endeavor.

Summary of Main Points

As you go through life, discern which experiences are worth attending to and which are best ignored. With concentration and clear intention, you can learn to pull your attention away from unwholesome thoughts and from the signs that trigger them.

You have the option of forgetting regrets, grudges, and stories that might otherwise sustain ill will or reactivate traumas. You have the ability to pause and stop unskillful actions of body, speech, and mind.

There are times when a skillful distraction is just the right cure—recite a verse of wisdom, undertake a compassionate act of service, or just sweep your floor. Patterns and habits that trigger defilements might ultimately need to be examined closely, but wait until you have supportive conditions for this inquiry.

Avoiding, ignoring, and forgetting certain thoughts can be useful strategies to refresh, balance, and free your mind. At times, a skillful withdrawal might be the wisest choice.

✎❀ *Setting Boundaries*

To strengthen your ability to turn away from states that you know will lead to harm or distress, notice when and how your energy goes out toward something (usually through craving, desire, resentment, or aversion) that is not worthy of your attention and time. Identify that entanglement and practice withdrawing your attention from its grasp. Refuse to be pulled into the vortex of fears, worries, grudges, anger, self-perceptions, shameful memories, regrets, fantasies, or attachments to views.

When obsessive thoughts are not fed by attention, they subside and wither away from lack of fuel.

Develop ways to set boundaries around your thoughts. For example:

▸ To support a peaceful sleep, you might tell yourself that you can let your worries go for now—you will deal with them tomorrow. Tonight, allow the mind to rest.

▸ Imagine there is a special box where you can store your worries and concerns to address at a more appropriate time.

▸ During a meditation session, make an agreement with your mind to focus on your meditation subject now, and promise that you'll address that worry or concern later.

- When you come home from work, resolve to leave thoughts, worries, and stories about work at the office. Enjoy a nice dinner with family or friends, or alone, free from obsessive identification with work.

- If you are burdened by guilt or past regrets, remind yourself that the past is gone. Then consider what you learned from your mistakes and give yourself permission to move forward in your life.

- If you torment yourself remembering your most embarrassing or shameful moments, do yourself a kind favor and just ignore that it happened—forget it! Everyone has been embarrassed now and then; everyone has acted in ways they are later ashamed of. If you have learned from the experience and are not continuing the disturbing behavior, find a way to shrug off the memory.

- If past traumas haunt you, remind yourself that it isn't happening now and connect with what is *actually* happening now. We can't change the past, but we can meet the present with wisdom, compassion, and mindful attention. The dangers that we fear are not usually actually happening in the present moment. Sense how mindfulness of the present can be a great shelter and refuge for the weary meditator.

CHAPTER 6

UNRAVELING THE CAUSES

Strategy #4—Investigate the Causes of Distraction

One has clearly seen causation; one has clearly seen
causally arisen phenomena.
—NUMERICAL DISCOURSES OF THE BUDDHA[67]

N O MATTER HOW real a familiar thought may feel, you can recognize that "this is just a thought." This powerful initial understanding opens the way for profound inquiry into the impermanent and empty nature of experience.

An ancient Buddhist story that predates the European folktale of *Chicken Little* (also known as *Henny Penny*) tells of a hare who is startled awake by the loud cracking sound of a jackfruit falling from a tree. Terrified, he runs through the forest shouting, "The world is ending! The world is ending!" Other forest animals panic. The entire forest seems to be in chaos. Hearing the fearful cries of the animals, a lion asks why they believe the world is ending. The snake says she heard it from the antelope. The antelope heard it from the frog. The frog heard it from the squirrel. Eventually the lion's questioning leads him to the hare. The lion uses "alternately gentle and strong words" to convince the frightened hare to return to the place where he was sleeping to find evidence for his belief that the world was coming to an end. When they reach the place, the hare realizes that what startled him was only a jackfruit falling to the ground. He understands his fears were unfounded and that the conclusion he drew was the result of misperception. The hare's delusion fades, and calm is restored in the forest.[68]

It is not easy to disentangle oneself from the web of misperceptions. In response to our distorted thoughts, assumptions, or memories, we may be overcome by fear, desire, or anger. Emotions can magnify misperceptions, making thoughts appear to be true. A wise and courageous friend might suggest rewinding those proliferating thoughts to examine the truth behind a mistaken perception, or we might need to be a compassionate friend to ourselves as we skillfully turn attention inward to peel back the layers of causes that produced our thoughts.

It is not necessary to interrogate *every* trivial thought that arises in the mind. Most of our thoughts will arise and disappear without causing any trouble—just brief blips in the complex field of attention. Only a few stubborn patterns might be worthy of intentional meditative investigation. In particular, toxic distractions and deep delusions will need to be understood and dismantled.

The investigation in this training will circle around two aspects of conditioning: (1) the impact of our associations with sensory stimuli and (2) the effect that an undercurrent of self-construction can have on perception. By understanding the causes that shape thoughts, you may find opportunities to intervene in your habits at a deep level, withdraw their fuel, and free your mind from the influence of harmful patterns.

This is a strategy of careful investigation. Whereas strategy #2, examining the danger, considers where the thought pattern is leading, strategy #4 emphasizes understanding the conditions that produce mental proliferation. This targeted meditative investigation into the causes that form thoughts should not fuel a further flurry of thinking, trigger the pain of past traumas, or reinforce stories of blame. Rather, it is an investigation into the ways you perceive and conceive of your experience. This inquiry homes in on the habitual views that fabricate the illusory sense of self and leads to liberating insights into impermanence, non-identification, and emptiness.

Ask yourself, "How did my story, belief, or habit come to be?" Look at the conditions that trigger your habits, feed unhealthy patterns, and perpetuate deluded thoughts. Avoid self-recrimination while genuinely wanting to understand, how did I get caught in this again?

⟡ *Brief Meditative Inquiry*

During your sitting meditation, the inquiry into the causes and conditions that affect thoughts must be brief. Ask a skillful question and pause briefly to sense your response. Then return to mindfulness of sitting and breathing or to your primary meditation practice.

Meditative investigation is powerful, but it should not devolve into extended self-analysis or personal explanations. It is enough to pose a pointed question, take a moment for curious observation, and nurture the desire to expose the underlying patterns that sustain the habit. Then, without becoming seduced into scrutinizing your personal history, fixating on a personality type, or assuming that past experiences will repeat, return your attention to present-moment mindfulness. Keep the inquiry brief so it does not lead to further distractions.

This strategy of investigating causes is traditionally described as giving "attention to stilling the thought-formation of those thoughts."[69] You can accomplish this by inquiring into the causes, conditions, and root tendencies that sustain thought. As you become mindful of the present quality of your attention, and your awareness of the dynamic force of causal relationships grows, fascination with the *content* of thoughts will diminish.

Processes that produce suffering or lead to the end of suffering are especially worthy of exploration. Events in the past may have been agreeable or disagreeable, fair or unfair, pleasant or unpleasant—the details of what happened are of only secondary interest. Primarily, this is an exploration of what we are doing *now* that allows past events to continue to distort our perceptions and limit our freedom. We are unearthing the layers of habit that influence our views, thoughts, and actions and become conditioning forces for future experiences.

RAIN = Recognize, Accept, Investigate, Not-Identify

A useful support for meditative investigation is the popular acronym *RAIN.*[70] *R* stands for "recognize"; *A* stands for "accept" or "allow"; *I* stands for "investigate" or "interest"; and *N* stands for "not-identifying" or "not taking it personally."

First, *recognize* what is happening. You might give it a label: planning, rehearsing, worrying, or whatever word describes the mental activity. Then, *accept* that this is the present condition. Notice whether a quality of acceptance is already present. Resistance, irritation, or manifestations of aversion are indications of a lack of acceptance.

Then *investigate* carefully. Perhaps ask yourself a few questions: "What causes and conditions produced this state of mind? What energies sustain thinking? Are these thoughts really expressing the truth of the situation? What is compelling me to repeat this entrenched habit? How does a thought appear to form my self-identity? What associated mental qualities never arise along with this thought?"

As your investigation deepens, you will increasingly see that you do not need to take this experience personally, and *non-identification* will arise.

Notice the emotions that accompany your thoughts. Sense the pleasant and unpleasant aspects of the experience. Feel the changing sensations in your body that accompany an emotion. Emotions come like waves. They occur, they're felt, they're known, and they pass. Notice how those emotions arise, observe the changes in the body while they are present, and see how they pass away or morph into something else.

If you notice that coarse states of anger have proliferated out of subtler feelings of disappointment, focus your mindful inquiry on the subtler cause—become aware of the disappointment beneath that anger. And then continue to inquire, what is feeding that disappointment? You might discover an uncomfortable sense of vulnerability, or a fear that "I might not be able to get what I need." Can you open to that raw discomfort?

Emotions often linger longer than the individual thoughts they feed because the body requires time to process the chemical manifestations of emotion. As your mindfulness becomes more continuous and your understanding deeper, the emotions will settle and cease to fuel thoughts. For example, an unmindful experience of fear might be sustained by thoughts of justification, remorse, or jealousy. Your perception might be affected by past traumatic experiences or biased comparisons. A *mindful* experience of fear, on the other hand, might highlight waves of changing sensations that manifest, dissolve, and disappear as the fear subsides.

In other words, fear can be known as present experience—it does not need to activate anxiety about the future or ruminations about the past. By observing how fear works, you will gain some measure of control over your response to it. Similar states of fear may arise later, but when they are mindfully recognized, they do not escalate. You are learning not to be afraid of fear but to see it mindfully, as you would any other mental experience.

The practice of *N* in the RAIN process, non-identification, matures through investigation of the causal dynamics of conditioned phenomena. We each have unique histories, but we don't have to take our stories personally. We each have our own emotions, but we don't need to believe that any emotional pattern is an inevitable description of who we are.

Make Non-Identification the Priority

To cultivate non-identification, investigate how past and present conditions influence your ingrained assumptions and reactions.

Do you feel ignored or take offense when a restaurant server passes by your table without taking your order—or do you hold compassion for the busy server? Do you feel slighted when a friend neglects to invite you to a dinner party—or do you value the other activities that you share together and accept that you shouldn't be included in every gathering? Do you feel elated when you are praised and prideful when complimented—or do you respond from equanimity with a simple "thank you"? Are you taking things personally—or are you dis-identifying from your self-centered experience and seeing it with clarity?

We often interpret events through the filter of "self-making" habits. Even minor events might trigger hurt feelings, cause rumination, or expose deep-seated attachments and past wounds. On the other hand, when you do not identify with experiences, you see clearly— events happen when conditions support them; things change; it's not always about you.

Caring for a loved one with dementia provides ample opportunities to practice not taking things personally. They forget names, recall events inaccurately, confuse identities, and ignore promises. When my grandmother confused her daughter with a distant cousin and her granddaughter with the nurse, we just smiled. It could have been upsetting if we had let her confusion trigger personal stories of being unappreciated or unrecognized, but no one took it personally.

One meditation student described a time when her mother, affected by dementia, cleaned a vase by dumping the tiny rocks it held down the garbage disposal. Standing by the sink with the vase in her hands, she had no idea how the rocks got into the drain. Rather than get angry, this student recognized her mother's intention to help and her joy in being useful—clearly her mother did not pour rocks down the drain to make the daughter's life more difficult. By recognizing that this accident was not an intentional attack, my student's sympathetic response enabled her to laugh about it and nurture conditions that lightened a bit of sadness during the painful years of her mother's decline.

Another meditation student was hiking on a favorite trail that had recently been "discovered" by a local mountain biking club. As he hiked along a narrow and steep section of the terrain, a group of cyclists from the club appeared around the bend. He stepped off the trail to a ledge to allow the bikes to pass, and they politely thanked him as they rode past. Internally, however, he simmered with rage. His mind silently fumed, "These people have taken over my trail!" Attachment and possessiveness fed his anger.

Noticing the absurdity of feeling possessive of a public trail, he recognized the self-focus embedded in his reaction. He was able to let it go and enjoy the hike. He shared, "It was a beautiful day. Before working with these strategies, my anger probably would have dominated my experience and I would have been unable to enjoy that hike." His skillful reflection became a cause for recognizing the many beautiful aspects of his nature walk, reinforcing appreciation instead of feeding greed and aversion.

Identification—whether with our views, experiences, thoughts, desires, or mental states—is a primary cause of suffering; non-identification is a cause for liberation. A deep and freeing investigation of mind will make non-identification a priority. As you see the causes that contribute to your restless distractions more clearly, you can root out any ingrained habit of taking things personally.

Exploring Ordinary Manifestations of Possessiveness

Notice when and how the sense of self arises in daily activities. Is there a felt sense you can recognize, or an elaborate story that your mind quickly narrates? As you navigate your daily activities, notice the way you perceive objects and discern the difference in perception when you claim something as your possession.

For example, as you approach a set of chairs where you frequently rest, notice whether there is one that you consider to be *your* place, *your* chair? Observe this experience of possessiveness. Learn how the sense of "mine-making" arises, is recognized, and affects your perceptions. How is your mode of meeting experience affected by repeated acts of mine-making? What are the characteristics of this possessive mind? What do you experience when you drop the possessive assumption and just see a chair?

Look throughout your daily activities for similar experiences when mine-making occurs and explore ways to loosen the grip on those attachments.

INQUIRE WITH CURIOSITY

While hiking in a forest, a friend approached a trail junction and noticed the antics of her mind. She was already tired, yet the unpleasant thought arose: I must take the trail to the left; it is best to choose the more difficult option. Behind that was another thought: I will not thrive unless I push myself. She described her understanding like this: "I had faced many similar choices throughout my life and suffered the same unpleasant thought that it was best to choose the more difficult option. I'd never before seen so clearly the underlying belief that I wouldn't thrive unless I pushed myself. At this moment I saw that this belief was unsubstantiated, and I intentionally abandoned it. I took the path to the right. Since that moment, my life has had more ease. I've stopped choosing the more difficult option simply because it is more difficult."

It is not inherently wrong to take the more difficult route, but we are not choosing it freely if we allow the belief "if I do not push myself, I will be a failure" to drive our actions. Assumptions like this restrict our flexibility to make wise choices in response to changing conditions. As a result, we may either underestimate the danger of a situation or overestimate our abilities.

By observing and investigating her thoughts, intentions, and beliefs regarding the decision to turn right or turn left, my friend expanded her appreciation of both difficult and easy trails. She also recognized the value of challenging herself and of choosing relaxation. Ultimately, she discovered greater latitude for discerning what a skillful choice might be in the myriad minor and major turning points of life.

Each of us lives with a personal identity that has been evolving since we were children. Our beliefs about ourselves affect how we perceive the world around us. Unfortunately, these beliefs often obscure reality and prevent us from seeing things as they truly are.

If you consider yourself to be an excellent tennis player but do not win a tournament, you might feel angry. If you don't have the money to buy the kind of clothes you believe you deserve, you might feel depressed. If you view yourself as smart, but fail to garner top honors in school, you might feel guilt. These emotional disturbances can create more extreme agitation, more suffering than the simple unpleasant feeling that arises from not getting what you want. If you do not question the validity of the personal identities you produce and cling to, you risk strengthening deluded concepts about who and how you are, rather than recognizing that *all* self-concepts are fabrications.

 Investigating Thoughts

You can investigate thoughts both during sitting meditation and in ordinary activities. Support your curiosity by asking yourself a few questions:

- ▶ What is giving rise to this thought?
- ▶ What beliefs are fueling this thought?
- ▶ What feelings or emotions accompany or condition this thought?
- ▶ What belief lies behind this thought?

If you notice strong emotion, identify the emotional state and observe corresponding sensations in the body.

Look deeply into your own experience and inquire:

- ▶ What is beneath this emotion?
- ▶ What is giving rise to this feeling?

Maybe a sensation in the body triggered fear—or a sound you heard, or something you saw. Perhaps a thought stimulated sadness or irritation. Maybe underneath sadness a sense of disappointment festers, nourished by more thoughts. "I didn't get what I wanted. Things didn't go my way."

Calmly and mindfully explore, examine, and inquire:

- What else is contributing to this mental proliferation?
- How did this come to be?
- What are the causes of this state, and then what are the causes of those causes?

The fundamental inquiry question is: What is going on here that is subtler, that I am not yet seeing clearly? At the core of this issue, is there craving, clinging, or aversion to change?

If you cling to self-concepts as though they were real, you might forget that all experiences change. You might not notice that your self-concept is a thought colored by attachment. A thirst for personal affirmation or social reinforcement of your identity might lead you to associate only with people who are willing to buy into your story. Minor differences of opinion might be misinterpreted as personal insults, and any situation that does not conform to your self-narrative might feel distressing.

We each live with our individual histories and unique aspirations in a world where we might struggle to get what we want and need. For mental habits resulting from deep trauma, solitary meditative investigation might not be appropriate. We might need the support of friends, teachers, therapists, medical professionals, or group contexts to look deeply into our experiences. There will be many times, however, when we can bravely and silently trace the interactions of our own thoughts, feelings, and emotions and free our mind from habitual ruts—both in the course of daily activities and when thoughts occur during meditation.

Everything Arises Due to Causes

As your practice matures, you will inevitably experience periods that are smooth and others that are turbulent. Your concentration will alternately settle into profoundly tranquil states or falter. Over two thousand years ago, the Buddha advised Venerable Anuruddha and his companions to discover what caused their concentration to weaken.

They had reported that their meditative perception would seem to be progressing, their concentration deepening, but after a while they would fall into distraction and be assailed by irritation, doubt, dullness, longing, elation, excessive energy, and other imperfections. The Buddha urged them, "you should discover the cause for that."[71]

Perhaps we would also do well to take the Buddha's advice and "discover the causes" that diminish our concentration and obscure our clarity. Instead of accepting the presence of defilements as inevitable, ask yourself what enabled them to arise and increase. Whenever an obstacle presents itself, be curious. Ask, what gave rise to that? What was happening just before your concentration began to diminish? For example, did your energy weaken, did a sound intrude, or did you feel an insistent itch in your scalp? Did your stomach rumble in hunger? Did a favorite tune pop into your mind? Did you feel proud that your concentration was developing well?

Whenever your concentration falters, notice what happened just prior. Not all causes occur in the preceding moment, but looking to the immediate past will expose many relevant causal conditions.

As the development of concentration cycles through phases of strengthening and then faltering, you can learn to recognize the conditions that cause concentration to diminish and find ways to quickly restore the conditions that strengthen concentration.

OUR = Observe, Understand, Respond

A famous Buddhist simile compares meditators who are skilled in the ways of their own minds with youths who examine their own faces in a mirror. If they find blemishes or smudges of dirt on their faces, they make an effort to remove them; if they find their faces are clear, they are happy. Similarly, meditators are taught to carefully examine the quality of their minds. If they find defilements, they should make efforts to remove them. If they find that their minds are pure, they happily continue to cultivate wholesome states.[72]

The acronym *OUR* can remind us of a three-step approach to working with our minds: *Observe* what is occurring in the mind. *Understand* the patterns. *Respond* wisely. The OUR acronym offers an alternative to the RAIN structure. Both OUR and RAIN are useful systems that give prominence to investigating and understanding the causal dynamics involved in habitual reactions. RAIN highlights the importance of acceptance and non-identification. It is particularly useful when we need to soften our tendencies toward blame, denial, or self-judgment; accept the conditions that are arising; and learn not to take those conditions personally. OUR provides a simple three-part process in which we observe and understand our response to a situation in order to improve future responses.

This book is itself organized in alignment with OUR. First, we learn to observe the mind and its patterns. Second, we understand the difference between wholesome and unwholesome states. And third, we apply the strategies for removing distracting thoughts as a skillful response.

Step One: Observe

We observe the mind as it encounters the six sense bases outlined in the Buddha's teachings. These are: seeing visual objects, hearing sounds, smelling odors, tasting flavors, touching tangible objects, and cognizing mental phenomena. For example, when you turn to look at a child riding his bike, you can notice that you are seeing. Notice that a movement of color caught your eye and notice how this perception affects your mood. Observe whether a train of thought proliferates and generates stories about your childhood. Take note if you start to contemplate giving a bike to your granddaughter for her next birthday.

An honest straightforwardness will enable you to gather the most accurate information about the mind and its habits. Ask, "What is the state of my mind right now?" You may realize that simply by asking the question you are opening to learning about yourself. Let go of any expectations about what you might find; trusting the unbiased observation, which characterizes mindfulness, will help you see things as they really are.

Through careful observation, you can gather information about the quality of your mind as it engages with experience. Is there longing, agitation, ill will, comparing, or fear? Is the perception accompanied by calm, curiosity, appreciation, joy, or concentration? How you relate to sensory stimuli and mental objects will determine whether you are caught by defilements or able to meet your experience with equanimity and wisdom.

The Buddha taught:

> . . . self-examination is very helpful for one to grow in wholesome qualities. One should ask oneself:
> (1) Am I often given to longing or without longing?
> (2) Am I often given to ill will or without ill will?

(3) Am I often overcome by dullness and drowsiness or am I free from dullness and drowsiness?

(4) Am I often restless or calm?

(5) Am I often plagued by doubt or free from doubt?

(6) Am I often angry or without anger?

(7) Is my mind often defiled or undefiled?

(8) Is my body often agitated or unagitated?

(9) Am I often lazy or energetic?

(10) Am I often unconcentrated or concentrated?[73]

Habitual mental ruts might seem to dictate the course of your life, just as a well-worn groove on a road might determine the path of a wheel. It takes attention and effort to get out of a rut, as it did for a student of mine who, after working for many years in a corporate job, found herself rushing through household chores and personal hobbies as if she had to meet an impending deadline. The habit of driving projects toward completion was so strong that she could not enjoy ordinary activities with her family. Wanting to change this pattern, she decided to try slowing down while pruning and composting in her garden. She was determined to do this in a leisurely, mindful manner, and to monitor her feelings, thoughts, and mental states.

Instead of her usual hack-clip-and-dump approach, she took the time to discover skillful ways to prune each plant. For example, careful attention when cropping a creeper vine enabled her to trim and unravel the vine without damaging the trellis. She learned when and how to prune back the apricot tree to maximize production the next year and how to detect the strongest shoots on the rosebushes. Each plant has a unique way of growing and propagating, and those simple discoveries brought joy and enthusiasm to the task.

When she caught her attention wandering off, she restored her mindfulness. When she felt the urge to rush, she intentionally paused, listened to the sounds of the birds and insects, took a few relaxed breaths, and felt the sensations of kneeling in the soft soil. Each time she noticed her mind dashing into the future, she shifted her focus and felt the weight of the shears in her hands or the warmth of the sun on her back. By repeatedly reestablishing mindfulness of present experience, she stopped allowing her mind to topple toward anticipating next year's successful harvest. These mindful pauses interrupted the habitual longing for the satisfaction that comes with finishing a project.

By employing careful observation, she recognized that this craving for completion was a "longing for being"—a craving for the identity of a successful person and the sense of security that she associated with being productive. At the root of many of her habits she found an assumption that the experience defined her self— that it said something about her value as a human being and who she was in the world. She was taking every project—even hedge pruning—personally!

Rushing to the finish line was not how she wanted to experience her life. There are times when she might still embrace a deadline and enjoy the pleasures of crossing a task off her to-do list, but she says she no longer feels compelled to hurry; she now enjoys being more present and less caught up in fantasies of future fulfillment.

Step Two: Understand

The second step is the learning phase of this process, in which you identify patterns, discern causes and effects, predict how the patterns will play out in hurtful or helpful ways, and comprehend the significance of your experiences. By understanding how the mind works, you can skillfully guide its development.

For example, if your mind assails you with thoughts of guilt or unworthiness, ask yourself, "What gave rise to this thought? What criteria do I use to gauge worthiness or guilt? Are they valid criteria? Am I able to assess each criterion accurately? Does this assessment support my welfare or hinder my development? How do those thought patterns affect my relationships, my choices in life, my experience of meditation?" When examined, many of the notions people have about themselves are found to be inaccurate, and they diminish when they are seen as just old patterns of thought.

✐ *A Written Dialogue with Yourself*

Write down one of your habitual thoughts, compose a question to ask yourself about it, and then answer your own question. Proceed through subsequent thoughts and develop a written dialogue with yourself. This inquiry practice can help you unpack the tangled web of beliefs and assumptions about the patterns that might otherwise ensnare your mind.

A student told me she liked the benefits of yoga but avoided doing it. At first, she was aware only of the basic thought, "I don't want to do this!" Attempts to simply abandon the thought were not effective, so she became curious and looked for deeper thoughts that seemed to give rise to her reluctance to practice yoga. Subtle, unpleasant bodily sensations associated with a rapid stream of assumptions appeared. "I need to be doing something else. I am not disciplined enough to succeed at yoga. It's no use, I've already lost so much flexibility. I have more important things to do. I should do something I will excel at." Working with the strategies for removing distracting thoughts, she consciously recognized this flurry of excuses as unhelpful.

She wrote down the stream of thoughts and posted it on her bedroom wall. Then, whenever one of the thoughts arose, she immediately recognized it as something she had already identified as unwholesome. With the clarity of that knowledge, it was easy to set those thought patterns aside. She was able to proceed with her yoga practice with less resistance and enjoy the benefits that she sought from the practice.

Step Three: Respond Wisely

Once you have observed and investigated an experience, you can decide whether a response is needed. An important facet of wisdom is discerning if, when, and how you should act with your body, speech, or mind, so that defilements are weakened and wholesome states are strengthened. You might respond by removing hindrances or by leveraging the stability of wholesome states for further growth.

If you discover a lingering unwholesome intention, take the opportunity to dispel it. For example, what is your attitude toward discomfort? Most people do not want to feel pain and react with aversion and resistance even to mild experiences of discomfort. If you tend to relate to pain in ways that increase mental distress, experiment with alternative responses. For example, if when you sit in meditation you experience tension in your shoulder, relax a bit and allow a sense of spaciousness to surround the unpleasant sensations. Recognize that the sensations and feelings are changing; they are impermanent.

When pain is intense, but you cannot alleviate it in the present conditions, try intentionally to notice a pleasant scent or a joyful sound so that pain does not dominate your perception. One wise attitude toward pain might be to simply be mindful of it as an unpleasant but natural condition of the body. If reactions arise, become aware of states of aversion and fear as simply present, but impermanent, mental states. Even brief moments of mindfulness can have powerful effects.

In medical research, placebos have been shown to substantially impact certain medical and psychological conditions, especially conditions that are affected by attitude and measured by subjective reports. A patient's expectations about the drug's effectiveness, as well as the context in which the treatment is offered, can influence the outcome. This is not mere fantasy or quack medicine; thoughts, views, and beliefs have been proven to influence the chemistry and healing activities of the body. Aware of the power of placebos, you can incline your mind toward thoughts that support health and healing. As illustrated by the earlier example of working with pain, even a slight adjustment to your attitude might be sufficient to decrease your suffering.

Once you clearly see your patterns, you can take an appropriate course of action. In the discourse on self-examination, the Buddha says, "If, by such self-examination, a bhikkhu knows: 'I am often given to longing, given to ill will, overcome by dullness and drowsiness, restless, plagued by doubt, angry, defiled in mind, agitated in body, lazy, and unconcentrated,' he should put forth extraordinary desire, effort, zeal, enthusiasm, indefatigability, mindfulness, and clear comprehension to abandon those same bad unwholesome qualities. Just as one whose clothes or head had caught fire would put forth extraordinary desire, effort, zeal, enthusiasm, indefatigability, mindfulness, and clear comprehension to extinguish the fire on his clothes or head, so too that bhikkhu should put forth extraordinary desire, effort, zeal, enthusiasm, indefatigability, mindfulness, and clear comprehension to abandon those same bad unwholesome qualities."[74] Do you feel this kind of urgency to improve the quality of your own mind?

A meditation student was struggling at her company with a new policy that she felt was misguided. Her mind was overcome with anxious thoughts; her anger was palpable, and she was having trouble sleeping at night. Convinced that the new policy would harm both her clients and fellow employees, she believed benevolence and compassion motivated her resistance. But as she investigated her proliferating thoughts further, she found that fear, conceit, and greed were also active. Her mind was not functioning solely in the service of developing ways to help her clients: she was also justifying her anger to resist a perceived threat to her professional identity.

As she lay awake rehearsing what she might say to her boss and clients, she decided to redirect her thoughts and investigate her mental process instead of remaining caught in rumination. She immediately noticed the interaction of emotions, thoughts, and physical sensations. She recognized the sense of gratification she gained by feeling morally superior and also the danger that ensued when her attitude fueled the defilements of anger and greed.

She reported, "When anger was present, my heart beat strongly. I felt hot and my muscles tensed. When sadness was present, my body felt heavy and the muscles felt sluggish. I saw that a huge risk of holding on to an identity is that it can continue to fuel anger. It leads to living with a constricted heart. I want to live with a heart that is open and loving."

As her understanding deepened, the coarser states of anger dissolved. She still felt some fear and conceit, but could watch the formation of identity without being totally invested in it. Using this opportunity to investigate her reaction, she discovered strong underlying views about how things should be done. This insight loosened the attachment to her own opinions and ways of doing things. After pondering what a *wise response* would be, she became more flexible and willing to work with the new policy for the benefit of everyone.

WHEN CONDITIONS ARE GOOD

Don't focus only on negative experiences as you examine the causes of thought-formations and the conditions they reinforce. Recognize positive or neutral thoughts as well. Emotions and bodily feelings can also be very useful. When you find your mind is pure, be happy that you have conducive conditions for deepening practice.

The Buddha instructs, "But if, by such self-examination, a bhik-khu knows: 'I am often without longing, without ill will, free from dullness and drowsiness, calm, free from doubt, without anger, undefiled in mind, unagitated in body, energetic, and concentrated,' he should base himself on those same wholesome qualities and make a further effort to reach the destruction of the taints."[75] When the mind is undisturbed, a wellspring of energy becomes available for deep spiritual practice.

There are times in life when you will have the interest, energy, and personal drive to tackle a difficult project, explore a tender issue, cultivate a valuable skill, or go deep in your meditation practice. There will be times when your mind is clear and you are free of identification with any situation. Supportive conditions for deep spiritual practice are not always present, so when you recognize that your inner resources are aligned with favorable external conditions, don't just loll in that temporary comfort or allow an initial success to engender complacency. Take advantage of conducive inner and outer conditions—use the opportunity to act for the benefit of yourself and others.

As you begin to reap benefits from this practice and gain confidence and faith in this path, it becomes easier to let go. When your mind is free from worry and anger, spiritual joy and tranquility are more accessible. This joy and calmness nourish deepening concentration. When your mind is well-concentrated for sustained periods of time, don't just revel in the pleasures of meditative bliss—leverage this hard-won stability to develop insight. The Buddha suggests that we recognize the support of wholesome conditions and with that support put forth a wholehearted effort to realize our goals. How can we best use the conditions that we are experiencing now?

Following the OUR plan, we mindfully *observe*, investigate to *understand*, and refine our *response* in the light of insight.

CALMLY NOTICE IMPERMANENCE

The process of personal discovery can be immediate, simple, and liberating. A few seconds of mindful investigation can be powerful enough to expose deeply conditioned habits, both in our worldly activities and interactions and in formal meditation. A brief inquiry into the formations of thought performed by a tranquil mind can penetrate entrenched habit patterns and produce a more accurate and useful perception of experience.

In the course of our daily lives, the mind will naturally distill the bombardment of sensory contacts into easily processed, fixed concepts, but time and again we confuse those concepts with reality. As we look meditatively into our physical and mental experiences, we recognize that every aspect of body and mind that participates in the process of cognition is changing.

When you smell an odor, does it appear continuous, or are you aware of brief breaks in the perception when your nose is not stimulated? Rapidly changing moments of experience tend to blur together as thoughts feed upon the stimulus. Concepts can create the impression of continuity by tying together many brief moments of sensory stimuli into identifiable, nameable entities. This process creates the appearance of continuous experience, and the illusion of continuity both obscures impermanence and concocts an illusion of self. Notice the many ways that thoughts embellish your story of self and are refreshed through your sensory encounters.

The most potent meditative investigation is supported by the stillness of a concentrated mind. The Buddha said, "Develop concentration! One who is concentrated understands things as they really are."[76] An agitated, unfocused mind will not have the steadiness to discern the subtle dynamics of the mind-body processes; it will not be capable of extrapolating the liberating implications from your entrenched perceptions. During your investigation of causes, conditions, and the qualities of your mind, you will need to maintain a significant degree of mental composure to prevent self-judgment, craving, or identity-attachment from hijacking your insights.

Meditative investigation is not concerned with personal narratives or the content of proliferating thoughts. We are not laying blame on our childhood conditioning or drafting policies to change social institutions. Instead, meditative investigation looks at the patterns that condition how we perceive, conceive, and relate to this present moment. This investigation of deeply ingrained thought processes should not fabricate more self-concepts or develop a story about "becoming the one who understands oneself." When your investigation of thoughts is supported by the agility of a concentrated mind, you will recognize the causes that produce habitual patterns and not weave them into another personal story.

FROM GROSS TO SUBTLE

Looking deeply into the mind to understand the source of your agitation can produce a profound calm. The simile used in the discourse on the Removal of Distracting Thoughts describes a man who is walking very fast and wondering: "Why am I walking so fast? Let me walk a little slower." And then he walks slower. After a while he thinks, "Why am I walking slowly? Maybe I'll stand." And then he stops and stands. Soon he considers the possibility of sitting, and he sits. Eventually he reclines. For each gross posture, he substitutes one that is subtler.[77] Similarly, when you notice the causes that fuel obstructive states, the grosser mental habits will be dispelled first, and then subtler types of thought will, in turn, emerge and dissipate.

Although realization can be swift, more often it is gradual. The simile indicates that one would progressively shift, stage by stage, from fast walking toward the serenity of reclining. In the same way, you might slowly recognize increasingly subtle layered views, flushes of emotion, physiological dispositions, personal habits, and social identities that distort your perceptions.

You can investigate the assumptions and emotional forces that give your thoughts the appearance of truth. By slowly tracing the formation of thoughts back to their sources, you can steer your way toward a beneficial and liberating path.

SUMMARY OF MAIN POINTS

By understanding the causal conditions that feed mental proliferation, you will be able to withdraw the fuel that feeds destructive thought patterns. Ask yourself, "What is fueling these thoughts? What feelings accompany these thoughts? What is going on here that is subtler?" Gradually track your thoughts back to find the beliefs or conditions that feed them.

Effective meditative investigation is supported by calmness and curiosity. It will focus on the dynamics of identification and attachment without veering into psychological analysis or spiraling into constructing new stories based on the results of the inquiry itself.

~ Asking Questions

At some point, you may feel the need to understand *why* and *how* you keep getting caught in the same persistent patterns. To learn more about the forces that feed habitual thinking, investigate the causes of the arising of repetitive thinking. When you notice an unwholesome pattern, look with curiosity; look incisively.

Ask yourself questions to reveal the *present* situation:

- ► What is the state of my mind right now?
- ► What is the quality of my attention right now?
- ► Is this pattern wholesome or unwholesome?
- ► How earnestly do I want to understand my mind?
- ► Are there physical sensations, temperature changes, movement, constriction, gestures, or postural changes that occur along with these thoughts?
- ► Are my emotions and thoughts feeding each other?
- ► Do I justify, explain, or feel gratified by these thoughts or feelings?
- ► Am I strongly attached to this thought? Do I believe it is true?
- ► How could I know whether this thought is true?
- ► What negative qualities of mind have become so familiar that they seem normal?
- ► Is there something I'm not seeing here?

Ask yourself questions to clarify *past* experiences and habitual patterns:

- ► How did this train of thought develop? How did I get here?

- ▸ What did it develop out of?
- ▸ What is feeding these thoughts?
- ▸ What is causing them to linger, proliferate, or arise again and again?
- ▸ What are the causes and conditions that gave rise to and nurture this pattern?
- ▸ Are these thoughts rooted in ill will, craving for sensual pleasures, or delusion?
- ▸ Was there an initial trigger for this story—perhaps a sight, sound, thought, or memory?
- ▸ What did I perceive just prior to engaging in the habitual pattern?
- ▸ What states frequently arise in my mind?

Ask yourself questions to consider potential *future* outcomes:

- ▸ Where is this mental process leading?
- ▸ What is this thought process serving?
- ▸ What would be "the danger" or the consequences of furthering the habitual pattern?
- ▸ Is there another way of perceiving this? Another perspective?
- ▸ What have I learned through this investigation?
- ▸ What is the quality of my mind during and after this kind of investigation?

Ask yourself many times a day, both during sitting meditation and in daily activities:

- ▸ What is the state of my mind right now?
- ▸ What is present and what is absent in my mind right now?

CHAPTER 7

SAYING NO AND MEANING IT!

Strategy #5—Apply Determination and Resolve

When, with his teeth clenched and his tongue pressed against the roof of his mouth, he beats down, constrains, and crushes mind with mind, then any evil unwholesome thoughts connected with desire, with hate, and with delusion are abandoned in him and subside. With the abandoning of them his mind becomes steadied internally, quieted, brought to singleness, and concentrated.
—MIDDLE LENGTH DISCOURSES OF THE BUDDHA[78]

I F YOU HAVE BEEN systematically working through the previous four strategies for removing distracting thoughts, you will only rarely need to apply the final strategy—bold determination, powerful effort, and courageous resolve. Stare down the defilement with the resolve that "This ends now!"

You'll rarely need it, but there might be times when your mind remains entangled in unwholesome thoughts, even after applying the previous strategies: replacing, seeing the danger, ignoring, and inquiring. If you continue to find yourself frequently engrossed in harmful thoughts during meditation or perpetuating unskillful actions in your daily routines, you might need the intensity of this fifth strategy to strike the final blow against the habit, regain your mental balance, refresh your aspirations, and recommit to your priorities.

When you are faced with a defilement that is hard to remove, don't give up. Some cooking pans clean easily, but occasionally vigorous scrubbing is required to remove baked-on debris. Extra effort may be needed to remove some habitual patterns, but the rewards that come from this work are profound. The Buddha explains, "When, with his teeth clenched and his tongue pressed against the roof of his mouth, he beats down, constrains, and crushes mind with mind, then any evil unwholesome thoughts connected with desire, with hate, and with delusion are abandoned in him and subside. With the abandoning of them his mind becomes steadied internally, quieted, brought to singleness, and concentrated."[79]

A Strong Man and a Sledgehammer

This strategy is traditionally illustrated by the simile of a strong man who seizes a weaker man by the head or shoulders and beats him down, constrains him, and crushes him.[80] The strong man is likened to the power of your resolve. Is your commitment strong enough to put an end to greed, hate, and delusion in your mind? Do you sense the inherent weakness of defilements that can survive only when you nourish them with habitual thoughts and actions? Are you confident that your mindfulness and wisdom are more powerful than your defilements?

I sometimes call this strategy the *sledgehammer approach*. A well-equipped tool chest will have a variety of tools, each useful for different tasks. Most tasks around the house do not require the sledgehammer. I would not use a sledgehammer to tap a picture hook into drywall, scrub food off dinner dishes, unscrew a faucet, or prune a rosebush. But if I need to break up concrete to repair the pipes beneath it, a sledgehammer will come in mighty handy—a screwdriver, scissors, or spoon will not get that job done. A sledgehammer is a useful tool that should not be scorned or feared; it has a purpose and a proper place in the array of available tools.

This strategy is the final step in the sequence for removing distracting thoughts—the last resort! You have already built a strong foundation for using it by nurturing the many meditative and investigative skills introduced in previous chapters. You already have many tools in your metaphorical toolbox.

By the time you reach this stage, you can clearly distinguish the wholesome from the unwholesome. You have developed antidotes to your familiar habits. You recognize the dangers and risks of indulging your patterns. You have tried starving them of energy by withdrawing your attention. You have understood the causes that gave rise to those habits. You have developed a bounty of meditative skills and clarified your priorities. You are confident in the knowledge that those distracting thoughts only thwart your aspirations. You sense the clarity that lies beyond the defilements. As the Buddha described, "With the abandoning of them his mind becomes steadied internally, quieted, brought to singleness, and concentrated."[81]

An intense application of effort can be powerful, but you must apply this method judiciously. It can be used to dismantle habitual obstacles and make room for wiser and kinder states in your worldly encounters and in your spiritual life. It can be a strong and assertive expression of energy, reserved for use when previous strategies have not been enough to subdue your most stubborn patterns. Using it, you can renounce the habits that inhibit your priorities and limit your growth.

In my own practice, I rarely need to explicitly employ this method. Every once in a while, however, a particularly sticky pattern refuses to acquiesce to the first four strategies. On those occasions I muster up an inner confidence to stare down the defilement with the resolve: This pattern ends now! More commonly, I see this strategy functioning as an undercurrent to my practice—an unwavering commitment to purify my mind in all actions and the confidence that I am standing in my own strength.

You may have made the commitment not to let defilements determine the course of your life, but now you must apply wisdom and energy. Having seen the situation clearly—both the rut formed by distracting habits and the potential for freedom—you can now say "no more!" and mean it. You can resolve not to produce even one more thought of aversion or greed. You can refuse to waste even one more minute of your life in deluded fantasies, personal excuses, or judgmental scenarios. You can stop allowing distracting thoughts that are conditioned by the past to determine your future possibilities.

Sensing your power to crush unwholesome thoughts can be invigorating, but if overused, this strategy might cause you to become hypervigilant, self-critical, or exhausted from the effort to vanquish every trivial imperfection. Remember, a sledgehammer is used only for appropriate tasks, and when wielding a sledgehammer, we must handle it with a certain amount of care. This strategy highlights the potency of commitment and faith.

To liberate your mind from distraction, you may need to apply persistent effort, but pick your battles wisely. Doing so will allow you to maintain your energy and draw encouragement from your successes.

Don't Doubt Your Own Strength

When you commit to a goal, you will likely feel energized. That energy can propel you forward with a dedication to your well-being and the well-being of others. You have acknowledged your starting point, where you hope to end up, and the path you need to take to get there. Each step adds power to your resolve until your full commitment will not permit you to stand idly by while defilements overtake your mind. You will live, as the Buddha urged a disciple, "with energy instigated for the abandoning of unwholesome states and the acquiring of wholesome states; [be] vigorous, energetic, and persevering with regard to wholesome states."[82] A vigorous pursuit of wholesome states can bolster your potential for becoming free from the defilements of greed, hate, and delusion. Continue to pursue your spiritual aspirations, and do not allow unwholesome states to stand in your way.

A successful assertion of strong will depends upon the clarity of your intention. You must know what is most important to you and then align your actions of body, speech, and mind with those intentions. What matters most to you? What are your priorities in life? What are your spiritual goals? When the Buddha pledged to continue practicing even if the flesh and blood of his body dried up, he was aiming for "that unsurpassed goal of the holy life." He applied his energy to achieve something he valued even more than his life. What do you value even more than your life?

This strategy of strong resolve expresses your heartfelt allegiance, your eagerness to take even a tiny step forward on the path to your goal. Calling upon your intention and connecting to your motivation will give you the strength to persist.

As you gather your forces to apply strong effort, keep your priorities in mind. If you slip up and find yourself once again lost in the habitual distraction, don't beat yourself up about it—restore balance to your mind. Respect your potential to train the mind; realign your energies with your commitments; reflect on what inspires you. Remember what you care most deeply about.

⁓ Clarify Your Goals

Consider what matters the most to you in worldly matters and your spiritual life. Then try to articulate your spiritual goals by composing a few sentences. To get started, try filling in the blanks in these prompt statements:

May I free my mind from _____.
I aspire to _____.
May I develop _____.
May I realize _____.
I dedicate myself to _____.

Then, construct ways of remembering your goals. You might create a collage of images and words that remind you of your priorities and values. Consider placing a photograph of a respected teacher or role model on your desk to remind you of admirable qualities. Perhaps pin a note on your wall with an aspirational quote or your personal intentions.

Integrity, determination, motivation, and commitment are not limited to meditation practice; they manifest beyond the meditation session to affect every decision, action, and relationship in your life. When you choose to say "no more!" you must mean it. If you waffle, you might weaken the new pattern that you want to create. Saying "no more!" and a moment later softening it into "maybe just this time" will undermine your capacity to apply determined effort. It would be like wanting to live with integrity and yet permitting yourself to steal, lie, or cheat "just a little." Capricious wishes and idealized hopes are not the ingredients of a powerful resolve.

You may have already seen success by applying the first four strategies and achieved upright and beneficial states of mind; however, if a habitual pattern has remained impervious to your efforts, don't stop there. Reinforce your commitment, get out the right tool, and finish the job.

When you are confident that you are developing the right skills for the task at hand, and you understand what the work entails, there should be no doubt that you will eventually succeed. Just as a lumberjack who strikes the trunk fifty times before the tree falls does not think that the first forty-nine blows were wasted, meditators must diligently train the mind, trusting that every moment of mindfulness is weakening the defilements. If the lumberjack made three blows and then scoffed "This axe isn't working for me" or "I can't do this," he would never fell the tree.

Diligence is the cornerstone of success. The Buddhist tradition chronicles many lifetimes of practice that prepared the Buddha for his awakening and tells of remarkable efforts made by the great disciples to purify their minds. The Buddha taught, "Whatever wholesome states there are, they are all rooted in diligence, converge upon diligence, and diligence is reckoned the chief among them."[83]

We must all be willing to diligently cultivate the mind without sabotaging ourselves with self-recriminations. Make the commitment, persist with your effort, and take every opportunity to weaken your hindrances one blow at a time until they fall away.

POSITIVELY NO!

Before you assert your strength, first confirm that your attitude is balanced and calm. Be sure that not even a tiny shred of hate or self-condemnation loiters in your mind. Energetic effort is not aggressive—avoid berating yourself for still being caught in that habit. Don't let the defilement of aversion creep in and corrupt the powerful application of your inner resources. Keep in mind the principles that you value. Take your stand motivated by compassion and wisdom. By having practiced the previous steps in this sequence, you are primed to formulate a strong determination that is informed by wisdom and that will support your aim.

For example, one meditation student shared,

> I was obsessed with playing online chess, and I could play it for hours on end. I was not only engrossed in the game while playing it, but chess games and puzzles frequently distracted me during meditation. The first four strategies for removing distracting thoughts did not seem to be effective at first glance. The classic antidotes didn't seem to apply: there was neither hatred to replace with loving-kindness, nor greed to replace with generosity.
>
> At first, I didn't see any danger in my love of chess. I considered chess to be a pleasant and harmless pastime. But I began to notice that it was a major distraction during meditation. And indulging this distraction weakened my commitment to liberation. I tried to withdraw my interest from thoughts of chess games, but my attachment was too strong. I felt flushed with pride each time I won a game, and I craved for that feeling.
>
> While working through the four strategies didn't overcome the immediate distraction, they helped strengthen my aspiration to free my mind. I began to view chess as a defilement. Perhaps for other people chess can be an innocent and intriguing game, but my obsession with it made it a problem. By perceiving it as a defilement, I gained a clear sense of purpose, and finally said "No!" to all forms of chess.
>
> I stopped playing, thinking, studying, and reading about chess. I removed chess from my life. This decision felt powerful. At first, I longed for the pleasures of the

game, but that longing was quenched by reflecting on my priorities. Soon enough, though, those distracting thoughts disappeared, and the sense of self that thrived on those addictions no longer controlled my decisions.

Look into your mind. If you are confident that your resolve is motivated by wisdom and not aversion, it may be appropriate to gather your wholesome strength and firmly say "no more!" to the defilement. Just as a pet owner is not angry when she sharply reprimands her dog when it dashes toward a busy street and responsible parents are not filled with hatred when they ground their teenager to curtail misbehavior, your assertion of "no more!" is not motivated by ill will but by the wise and caring desire to protect your mind from defilements. Set healthy boundaries for your attention; curb your thoughts. Don't allow your mind to visit its habitual haunts even one more time.

The Buddha was not afraid of the task before him, nor did he doubt his ability to effectively apply his effort. He declared,

> "Through diligence have I won enlightenment, through diligence have I won the unsurpassed security from bondage. If you too, O monks, will struggle unremittingly and resolve: 'Let only my skin, sinews and bones remain; let the flesh and blood in my body dry up; yet there shall be no ceasing of energy till I have attained whatever can be won by [human] strength, [human] energy, [human] effort!'—then you too will soon realize through your own direct knowledge, in this very life, that unsurpassed goal of the holy life."[84]

The Buddha described what he needed to achieve his goal: diligence, resolve, and effort. Though the struggle to free the mind may seem daunting, we might find inspiration in the example of this remarkable human being who made the effort and succeeded. We too can make the effort, and perhaps we too will gain the direct knowledge of liberation that is supported by our diligence.

༄ A Meaningful "No!"

If unskillful thoughts continue to arise, you may need to confront them with more energy. If you find yourself repeatedly caught in a pattern of craving, a flurry of worry, a proliferating series of stories, or chronic planning fantasies, say "no!" to those thoughts and mean it.

Try it. Simply but clearly, say, "No! Enough of that. It is not good for me and I simply will not entertain it any longer!" Watch the mind for some time, reflect on the wisdom that brought you to the certainty that those thoughts are not helpful, and repeat the resolve again if needed.

EXCESSIVE EFFORT MAY BACKFIRE

If you have found success in life by applying brute force—pouncing on what you desire and pushing away what you don't like—you might have brought that driven, ruthless energy into your meditation practice. If so, be careful; you could be making meditation more difficult and exhausting than it needs to be. Facial pain, jaw tension, and headaches are common signs of excessive and unbalanced effort.

Some people respond well to consistently applied forceful exertion, while for others this can trigger an inner rebellion against their good intentions. No one likes feeling coerced, not even if we are convinced that it is in our best interest. Rather than demand that your mind conform to an idealized and unrealistic vision of a habit-free state, invite yourself to pause. Take a breath and then reaffirm the intentions that guide the best choices you make in life. Recollect your priorities. Trust your potential to experience the deep peace and sublime joy that is possible for a mind free of restless agitation. Consider the quality of effort that you need to wisely meet this moment, right here and now.

This practice sequence for removing distracting thoughts should not culminate in a duel in which you are, so to speak, fighting your defilements to the death. Reliance on harsh, demanding, or judgmental thoughts is likely to backfire. Research has shown that subjects who overuse willpower to combat cravings may initially abandon the attachment, but if confronted soon thereafter with a similar temptation, they are likely to succumb. Giving in to the second temptation may seem like a justifiable reward for the previous restraint or offer solace for passing up the initial attraction.[85]

Throughout this training you have been learning about your own habits and developing the ability to apply your energy skillfully. You have developed many skills, and do not need to rely solely upon the power of your determination. It is often more effective to fortify your commitments with wisdom than to make excessive effort. Confirm that your intentions are clear and reflect on the potential positive outcome you seek. You have developed a wide range of skillful practices; you are capable of giving your full energy to what you deeply value. As you negotiate the nuances of daily choices, sensory perceptions, mental habits, and spiritual aspirations, trust that a full and balanced energetic commitment will bring you joyfully closer to your goals.

SUMMARY OF MAIN POINTS

This final strategy, strong determination, is your last resort when the other four strategies have been applied but a more forceful response is still needed. You can now say "no!" to that defilement or habitual pattern—and mean it. This strategy must be applied sparingly, or you risk exhausting yourself from excessive effort or even backsliding into aversive states. Strive to apply effort skillfully—neither too little effort nor too much. Wholehearted resolve commits your full allegiance to the values you have wisely prioritized, and asserting your determination aligns your thoughts with your goals.

CHAPTER 8

APPLYING THE FIVE STRATEGIES

A Complete Training Sequence

*One wields mastery over the mind, one does not
let the mind wield mastery over him.*
—MIDDLE LENGTH DISCOURSES OF THE BUDDHA[86]

EACH OF THE STRATEGIES presented in this book plays a unique role in this training. Together, they form a synergistic practice system that overcomes distractions and nurtures meditation skills. These strategies are traditionally taught in a particular order and work together as a developmental sequence. The skills and understandings developed in the earlier steps support the effectiveness of the later steps.

By following the sequence step by step, you lay a reliable foundation for success. Systematic practice avoids the pitfalls that might occur if an overly eager practitioner were to skip the initial strategies in favor of later strategies in the series. The earlier strategies develop skills, knowledge, and maturity that help one to successfully apply the later strategies.

If, for example, you were to apply energetic resolve (strategy

#5) before understanding causality through strategy #4, the influx of energetic effort could produce excessive mental pressure, self-judgment, or aversive reactions. If you try to ignore habitual distractions (strategy #3) before you have seen the danger posed by those distractions (strategy #2), you might only suppress the defilements, which may reemerge somewhere else. If you try to examine the danger (strategy #2), before you have nurtured a healthier alternative to the distracting thought (strategy #1), you might despair that your patterns seem intractable.

It is more skillful to train your mind systematically. Only after you are familiar with the full series would you begin to apply the strategies in fluid and creative ways.

The first strategy of replacing unwholesome thoughts with more wholesome alternatives often effectively dispels distraction. Just because it comes first does not imply that it is weak. In fact, you may find that this initial practice is all it takes to displace an unwholesome thought and to cultivate mindfulness and concentration.

If a defilement is persistent and the first approach to it does not work, simply move to the next strategy in the sequence. Continue working step by step through the strategies until the distraction abates.

As you master these skills, you will not always need to apply the strategies in the traditional order. With experiential knowledge, you will learn to sense which ones will dislodge a given habit pattern—irrespective of the sequence—and intuitively employ them to effectively free your mind.

How to Apply All Five Strategies to a Pattern of Anger

One meditation student described her use of these strategies—replacing, examining, ignoring, investigating, and resolving—to dislodge a particularly sticky pattern: a tendency to get angry at her partner.

This aversive reaction frequently occurred when her partner argued with other family members. She reported,

> When I see that my mind is inclined toward anger, I often use replacing (strategy #1). I may reflect on my partner's positive qualities or I may intensify my mindfulness by applying a mental note every second or two to connect with whatever is in my awareness. If anger lingers while I am using the mental noting technique, I will note it as "anger." I find that this practice usually prevents my mind from obsessing on angry thoughts and they eventually dissipate.
>
> To increase my dedication to eliminating this thought pattern, I reflect on the dangers (strategy #2). I remember painful results from previous occasions when I indulged the anger. I also remember positive outcomes from times when I've let go of the anger. Reflecting on the danger does not usually stop this thought pattern, but it inspires me to continue to work with replacing (strategy #1) or ignoring (strategy #3).
>
> I can sometimes prevent anger from arising by reminding myself that her arguments with other people are not my business (strategy #3). It helps that we have agreed that I am not obliged to participate, take sides, mediate the dispute, suggest compromises, or serve as the peacemaker in the family. Remembering that it is not my business usually is effective at preventing or dispelling this angry reaction.
>
> But when I hear yelling, the loud voices attract my attention. Then, I might busy myself by doing something else (strategy #3), remove myself from the room (strategy

#3), or focus my attention on physical sensations that arise as I hear their voices (strategy #1).

When I am calm enough and am in a place that feels private and safe, I reflect (strategy #4). I have become aware that these arguments trigger memories from my early childhood of chaos, helplessness, and fear. When I realize that the underpinnings of my anger toward my partner actually have nothing to do with her, my belief in those thoughts diminishes, and faith in the rightness of abandoning anger increases.

As I investigate, sometimes I sense how my intense reaction reinforces notions about who I am in this relationship and the kind of person I am in this world. My reactions create a story about me; it is a separate story from the present conflict that they are arguing about. I have seen that when I invest in this self-story, I feel disconnected, isolated, and unable to experience deeper intimacy. But when I don't invest energy in the self-story, this reactive anger tends to fade away, and soon enough, the volume of their voices quiets down too. Their arguments rarely last very long, but my anger and fear can last much longer than their arguments if I am not diligent.

Over time, I have come to understand this anger, and learned to soften its impact on my mind and relationships. But my reactivity has not completely ended. Sometimes the arguments occur in a busy situation and I just don't have the time or mental bandwidth to systematically apply the first four strategies. But if I can catch it quickly, a brief recollection of my commitment to abandon this harmful pattern, combined with a firm statement to myself—"no, stop!"—can be remarkably effective (strategy #5). Because I have practiced the previous four strategies and developed faith that stopping is the right thing to do, just reminding myself to stop can be enough to prevent anger from gaining momentum.

When anger is not agitating my mind, concentration develops more readily in my daily meditation practice. When my mind is concentrated, I experience a wonderful quality of pleasure; it is a subtle sense of contentment and enthusiasm. I sense my mind saturated with calm, and equally eager to understand. At these times, my desire for freedom is strong and it also seems possible. This calm enthusiasm energizes my commitment to continue to practice.

As this student has discovered, once you have become skilled in these strategies for replacing, examining, ignoring, investigating, and resolving, it will not always be necessary to adhere to the traditional order. This system is flexible, and while it is important to approach the strategies in order in the beginning, you will eventually be able to intuit which approach will effectively counter your current distraction. Your understanding will inform and shape the skillfulness of your effort.

Right Effort

Whatever the strategy you employ for working with your thoughts, understanding and practicing with the principle of right effort will support your success.

Right effort in the Buddhist tradition is usually described as having four facets:

> The effort to avoid unwholesome states that have not yet arisen;
> The effort to abandon unwholesome states that have already arisen;

The effort to cultivate wholesome states that have not yet
arisen;
The effort to maintain wholesome states that have already
arisen.[87]

We do our best to deal with the present situation and then reflect
on the results of our efforts. We make skillful adjustments, try again,
and again reflect on the results. Freedom is in your response to what
is happening now. Do not wait for everything to be perfect—you
might learn the most from your biggest challenges.

To determine whether a practice is appropriate and effective, do
not assess its value based on the pleasure-pain continuum or the
ease-struggle scale, but on its ability to lead away from harm and
suffering. The Buddha described four kinds of actions: (1) deeds
that may be disagreeable to perform and prove harmful, (2) deeds
that may be disagreeable to do and prove beneficial, (3) deeds that
may be agreeable to do and prove harmful, and (4) deeds that may
be agreeable to do and prove to be beneficial. He teaches that one
should perform deeds that are beneficial, not those that are harmful,
regardless of the affective quality associated with the action.[88]

In another context, the Buddha taught that "when you know
for yourselves: 'These things are unwholesome; these things are
blameworthy; these things are censured by the wise; these things,
if undertaken and practiced, lead to harm and suffering,' then you
should abandon them. . . . But when you know for yourself: 'These
things are wholesome; these things are blameless; these things are
praised by the wise; these things, if accepted and undertaken, lead
to welfare and happiness,' then you should live in accordance with
them."[89]

Some beginners expect immediate results. After all, meditation
looks easy—just sitting quietly. Other meditators adhere to the philosophy that effort is inherently virtuous—there is no gain without pain. Both ideas are wrong: there will be times when you will

really need to stretch yourself and times when relaxing is the ideal response.

For some people, meditation produces states of profound relaxation; the mind is infused with sublime ease. If you become enchanted with relaxation, however, and only do what feels easy or comfortable, you may become lazy. Laziness can be a huge obstacle for meditators because it can reinforce a reluctance to change habits, even obviously painful habits.

On the other hand, one who is habitually harsh or self-critical might need to relax before skillfully applying vigorous effort. It is useful to accept the present moment and learn to enjoy the simple experience of being mindful before striving to improve ourselves. Don't be deceived into thinking that success comes solely through relaxation or pleasurable states, but if distractions persist, you can apply gentle but still assertive ways to free your mind from those unwholesome states and refocus your attention on your aspirations.

In daily situations, you might employ gentle resolves as prophylactic measures to avoid triggering anger, envy, pity, or jealousy. Before walking into that meeting, opening that letter, or returning that phone call, resolve not to allow angry thoughts to arise in your mind. If unwholesome thoughts should sneak in anyway, quickly cut them off with the clarity of your resolve. Support your intentions with what might be called "a little oomph." Apply strong effort when you need it, but appreciate incremental shifts and also enjoy the times when you can just relax.

⌒❧ A Prophylactic Resolve

Choose a common but minor situation in which habitual defilements tend to influence your reaction. You can work with more critical situations as your skills develop. You might start with irritations like waiting in a long line at the post office, installing new software, or another ordinary situation that triggers frustration.

Before you enter the situation, consciously reflect upon your attitude and motivation. Consider how you might engage with it so you maintain a balanced mind and intact self-respect. What would it take for you to be fully present, remain aligned with your values, act for the benefit of yourself and others, and avoid dwelling on the outcome in the future?

For example, when waiting in line at the post office you might resolve not to become upset at others if the line is moving slowly, but instead generate loving-kindness for everyone in the building. If you need to install new software, you could welcome this opportunity to nurture patience and flexibility while improving your system. Make a firm commitment not to entertain resistance to this chore; undertake the task step by step; give it the time it requires; and banish resentment from your mind.

By anticipating ordinary frustrations, you can take proactive measures to mitigate the force of habit and stay firmly grounded in wholesome intentions.

A Meditative Review of This Training

First, establish mindful attention. Feel your body sitting. Become aware of your posture. Align your spine with gravity. Sensing the support of the seat and the floor, allow any excess tension to release from the muscles. Move your attention through your body from your head to your feet, mindful of the presence or absence of sensations in various parts of your body. Let your attention settle calmly and easefully into the present experience of feeling your body sitting and breathing.

Whether you focus more on the body, the breath, feelings, or mind, there will inevitably be times (assuming you are not already perfectly enlightened) when thoughts distract you. What can you do about distracting thoughts?

Next, know thought as thought. Reviewing the approaches outlined in this book, remind yourself that a thought is simply a thought; it is a discrete mental event. Simple mindfulness of the process of thinking often results in disenchantment with the content of thought.

Next, is it harmful or helpful? If thoughts continue, determine whether they are wholesome, such as generous, equanimous, honest, or wise thoughts; or unwholesome, such as envious, angry, selfish, or lustful thoughts. While unwholesome thoughts may need a vigorous response to prevent the defilements from spreading, simply resting back and observing thoughts arise and pass away might be a sufficient response when thoughts are wholesome and your attention is not entangled in them.

Finally, use the five strategies. If you find that unwholesome thoughts persist, you can choose to proceed through the five strategies presented in the discourse on the Removal of Distracting Thoughts.[90]

Strategy #1—Replace Unwholesome Thoughts with Wholesome Thoughts

Intentionally replace the unwholesome thought with a wholesome alternative. For example, you might abandon aversion by replacing it with loving-kindness. You might let go of desire and lust by contemplating impermanence. Any unwholesome state can be replaced with mindfulness of the present moment. In fact, merely bringing attention to present experience will likely dispel most hindrances and distracting thoughts.

By practicing in this way, your mind may become steady, calm, and concentrated, but certain entrenched distracting thoughts might endure. You might be dutifully following this initial mindfulness instruction: notice when the mind wanders and bring attention back to present sensations. Again and again the mind might wander. After dozens, hundreds, or thousands of times, you might sense that another approach is needed.

Strategy #2—Examine the Dangers of Distracting Thoughts

Examine the danger in the distracting thoughts. What danger could entertaining this distraction pose? What reward do you seem to be getting out of it? What are the hidden costs? If you indulge this distraction, will the harm or happiness it brings be greater in the long run? Do you want to go in the direction this is leading you? Remember the image of the fishhook and try to discern if there is a danger lurking underneath the tantalizing bait.

The very effort to see the danger can produce dispassion toward the thoughts. The distraction will often subside, and your mind will become balanced, quiet, and concentrated.

Strategy #3—Avoid It, Ignore It, Forget It

If distracting thoughts linger, they may be feeding on your attention. Employ strategy #3—withdraw your attention, forget them, ignore them. If regrets about past incidents persist, remind yourself that the situation has ended; it is not present now. If worry about the future is obsessive, recognize that it is a fantasy; it is not present now. If thoughts are overwhelming, take your mind off your troubles by enjoying healthy alternative activities. Practice directing your attention wisely; calmly cultivate mindfulness with a simple meditation practice such as observing sensations while sitting and breathing.

Strategy #4—Investigate the Causes of Distraction

If unwholesome trains of thought persist, explore the subtler inner dynamics with strategy #4—inquiry into causes. Explore the interaction of your thoughts, feelings, and emotions. Reflect on the causal conditions that fuel unwholesome habits. Through gradual, careful investigation, you will discover what the distracting thoughts are feeding on.

Follow the clues as they reveal subtle dynamics of your conditioning and discover striking insights into the construction of your sense of identity. From the initial delusion that posits an idea of self, the world conspires to reinforce it.

Your opinions and personal preferences are defined by that concept of self. Craving protects that sense of self. Meditative investigation can gradually expose the ingrained patterns that fabricate formations of I, me, and mine and fuel a host of deluded thought patterns. When severed from their fuel, the stories of self can dissolve, concentration can develop, and deep release can occur.

Strategy #5—Apply Determination and Resolve

Every once in a while, an ingrained toxic thought pattern stubbornly persists even after dosing it with the full array of these meditative strategies. By this point in the training, you understand the underlying causes. Recognizing it as a conditioned pattern, you do not take it personally. You have checked, and neither anger toward that pattern nor self-hatred festers in your mind.

You are prepared to tackle it with strategy #5—energetic resolve. With a clear and levelheaded determination, you decide that this pattern must stop now! Say "no!" to that defilement. Commit powerfully to not wasting another moment of your life feeding that toxic pattern.

Just one clear and resounding "no!" may be enough for the thoughts to dissolve. Or you might need to assert this determination a few times and cycle through one or more of the strategies to allow the momentum of the conditioned pattern to dissipate. You might cycle through the strategies rapidly, simply refreshing the understandings that each perspective highlights. At other times, you might work slowly and patiently with these tools, as you learn about the tendencies of your own mind.

Gradually, the beauty of your deeper commitments will fill the space that opens in the wake of freedom from conditioned patterns. Distracting thoughts will fade away and your mind will grow still, concentrated, composed, and unified—organized to support your spiritual path, and ripe for profound insight.

These powerful strategies free the mind from habitual patterns and clear the path for liberating insight.

CHAPTER 9

MASTERING YOUR MIND

Moving toward Liberation

This bhikkhu is then called a master of the courses of thought.
He will think whatever thought he wishes to think and he will not
think any thought that he does not wish to think.
—Middle Length Discourses of the Buddha[91]

THERE IS A TALE of a hermit who painted an amazing mural of a tiger on a cave wall. Just as he put the finishing touches on the eyes and stepped back to admire his work, he became terrified and dashed out of the cave. The painting was so realistic he feared that the tiger might attack him! Some readers might be amused by such a reaction or believe themselves immune from the power of their thoughts, but we have probably already seen that we can react emotionally and sometimes intensely to the fantasies that we create.

Thoughts color the perceptions of the unenlightened mind. We may have some intellectual understanding that our thoughts are not objective reality, that they are merely fabrication; however, unless we see thoughts clearly as *thoughts*, they will continue to affect our perceptions, views, decisions, and actions. Every time we become angry over an imagined conversation with our boss, worry as we rehearse a response to family news, or anticipate happiness at completing a home improvement project, we are looking into the eyes of a creature we have created and responding as though it were real.

Liberation requires letting go of the illusion that we exist as a permanent self, an observer, a witness, or the controller of activities. Self-grasping is not abandoned through effort, but by understanding that the illusion of self is constructed through layers of mental habits, misperceptions, and attachments. Some people think that just sitting for hours on the cushion will bring liberation. But this will not happen if we are simply focusing on sensations and abandoning thoughts. Some people think that behaving more ethically and thinking kinder thoughts will bring liberation. Although behaving ethically is a necessary condition for liberation, it is not sufficient.

One lesson I have learned from four decades of practicing Buddhism is that inner transformation does not come about by trying to form a better identity or gain a special experience. It goes far beyond self-improvement projects. Powerful liberating understandings occur by directly experiencing the "nots"—not-clinging, not-self, not-mine, not-fabricated, not-identifying.

We are not cultivating a grander, more polished identity. Letting go of habits and unbinding the mind from the forces of delusion are the route to freedom. Liberation comes not from *becoming*, but from *letting go*.

Silent retreats, where we step outside the usual patterns that structure our daily existence, provide an intensive and efficient context for shedding the burden of becoming. During that retreat period, you do not have to be the mom, dad, teacher, nurse, employee, boss, and so forth. You do not need to carry a self-image around. There are no phone calls or worldly contacts that would trigger identity construction. Retreatants do not need to create the impression of being smart, savvy, stylish, popular, articulate, or strong. A great weight is lifted as we walk through the door to the meditation hall; there is a real joy that comes from dropping all that self-making.

Intensive insight meditation retreats can develop a powerful momentum of mindfulness. However, even if you cannot attend a retreat, diligent practice of these methods in your daily life can result in profound understandings and vital skills that gradually clear away habitual reactions, improve your daily encounters, cultivate concentration, and incline the mind toward liberation.

Thoughts Are Not Reality

Through letting go of harmful or habitual thought patterns, you may experience a transformative insight into not-self. The insight is not an attack upon an actually existing personal identity, but a recognition of an absence that was always there. It is like realizing that although a movie may be engrossing and entertaining, it is just a creative production—not reality. It is the recognition that even though the world of experience appears vivid, it does not last and it is not under our control—"it is empty of self."[92]

A film of a storm does not leave the movie screen wet; robbers do not leave bullet holes on the screen; characters in romances do not live happily ever after. We may know this intellectually, yet time and again, we are seduced into the story and forget that it is merely a fictional drama performed by actors and edited in a studio.

Until we see our personal stories as just a series of thoughts rather than investing them with the belief that they constitute a "self," we'll remain attached to our own dramas. We might find ourselves in the starring role of a comedy or tragedy—perhaps the hero, maybe the victim. We might become so engrossed in personal narratives that our hearts race as angry thoughts enumerate the ways we feel wronged; we might experience a pleasurable rush by imagining we won a prize; we might sink into depression when we judge that our achievements have fallen short of expectations. Whether the story is played out on a movie screen or in the mind, the story is fiction.

If you think of a dinosaur, you can be sure that does not mean there is a dinosaur in front of you! It is no more real than any other thought. If you remember an argument that you had with your sister or worry about a problem at work, those events are not actually happening in real time. In the present moment, you are only imagining them. If believed in and attached to, those thoughts might feel real, generate emotions, produce a physiological response, and forge an illusory sense of identity. Still, they are just clusters of thoughts that exist in your mind. Your self-concept is no more real than the thought of a dinosaur or a painted image of a tiger.

It might seem as though attachment to self-concepts is the inevitable way of the world, but there is an alternative.

IN A MOMENT OF CONTACT

You have been learning to examine how your mind functions in a moment of contact. We experience countless momentary processes—seeing, hearing, smelling, tasting, touching, and thinking—that are interpreted and bound together through conditioned processes of perception. One of the Buddha's great disciples, Venerable Mahākaccāna, describes a sequence of events that can lead to mental proliferation:

> Dependent on the eye and forms, eye-consciousness arises. The meeting of the three is contact. With contact as condition there is feeling. What one feels, that one perceives. What one perceives, that one thinks about. What one thinks about, that one mentally proliferates. With what one has mentally proliferated as the source, perceptions and notions tinged by mental proliferation beset a human with respect to past, future, and present forms cognizable through the eye.[93]

This process occurs countless times a day, constructing the story of our lives out of distorted interpretations of sensory data and fragments of mental impressions.

 Can You Find the Agent We Call Self?

When you have an intention to shift your posture during meditation—turn away from a cold draft, scratch an itch, look at your watch, adjust your seat, examine the desire to move—what decides to move? You might say "I" decided to move, but which aspect of mind conditioned the desire to move? Was it fear, restlessness, compassion, desire?

After a meditation session, reflect on some additional questions: Are you really the aspect of mind that prompted the movement? Do you really claim that as "I"?

When you make the decision "I will not move," which aspect of mind conditions the decision to remain still? Is it confidence, resolution, determination, embarrassment, fear, pride, commitment, or desire to achieve?

Instead of assuming the existence of a self that is the deciding agent behind choices, notice the conditioning relationships that affect consciousness. When looking at your choices as the interplay of conditioned factors, can you find an actual agent to call your "self"?

We encounter sensory and mental stimuli, we feel, we perceive, and we think about our experiences. If we identify with an experience, our thoughts may construct a sense of self in relation to the experience. Proliferating thoughts will embellish the story of self and define how this emergent sense of self should orient to the world of experience. By imposing preferences of favoring or opposing, liking or disliking, we create personal meaning out of impersonal sensory impressions.

Habitual patterns of thought create narratives starring *me* in the past, *me* in the future, and *me* as I exist right now. But outside the story, there is no self. The concept of self arises when we cling to perceptions and thoughts. If, on the other hand, those moments of contact and feeling are met with mindfulness and wisdom, we will simply be aware of present experiences—such as seeing a visible object, hearing a sound, tasting a flavor, smelling an odor, experiencing a sensation, or thinking a thought. We would be aware, engaged with our lives, and able to analyze, reflect, decide, plan, and use our minds wisely.

CONSTRUCTION OF IDENTITY

When we can observe the unfolding interaction of conditioned psychophysical processes without converting present experience into a personal story, we will avoid the cascade of habitual reactions that serve as the building blocks for the concept of self.

Whenever I discover that I am identified with experience, I like to ask myself a brief question: Really? Am I really that? Really, is that experience mine? I have asked the question hundreds of times, and I have not yet found anything stable enough to claim, "Yes, indeed, this is really myself. Always and forever me." I only find changing psychophysical processes—momentary formations of grasping that arise to form an impression of self.

The chief disciple of the Buddha, the Venerable Sāriputta, was once asked, "What now is identity?" In response, Venerable Sāriputta points to five aggregates—these are the functions of body and mind that enable experiences to be known. If affected by clinging, they construct identity; but when not affected by clinging, they do not become the basis for identity. He says,

These five aggregates subject to clinging, friend, have been called identity by the Blessed One; that is, the form aggregate subject to clinging, the feeling aggregate subject to clinging, the perception aggregate subject to clinging, the volitional formations aggregate subject to clinging, the consciousness aggregate subject to clinging. These five aggregates subject to clinging have been called identity by the Blessed One.[94]

These five aggregates can be summarized as (1) the experience of our material bodies, (2) feelings, (3) perceptions, (4) volitional activities, and (5) the knowing of these experiences. We construct identity through attachment to our bodies, reactivity to feelings, misperception of sense impressions, identification with intentions and thoughts, and reification of the process of knowing. Venerable Sāriputta does not deny that individuals experience their lives in unique ways; still, through this model of the five aggregates, he highlights the crucial role that clinging to experience plays in forming identity.

A fabricated identity creates the appearance of a fixed concept of self that appears to have a place to stand. One then seems to become the owner, observer, knower, or experiencer of events that are filtered through one's personal perspective. But I would ask again: Really? Am I really that? Is there really an entity who is doing the observing, or is there simply a dynamic activity of observing occurring? Is a conditioned process of cognition occurring, or is there a self behind the action which is claiming to know? Are changing events recognized as such, or has a fixed role of being the witness formed?

Practice meeting each moment without identifying with personal stories that could distort perception. By scrutinizing experience and exposing it as empty of self, you will develop the skills of a meditator who, as the Buddha taught, "does not recognize either a self or anything belonging to a self in these six bases for contact. Since he does not recognize anything thus, he does not cling to anything in

✎ Identify the Five Aggregates as They Function in Sensory Encounters

As your observing powers increase with mindfulness practice, attention will more frequently meet present-moment experiences. Without the drama and distraction of elaborate stories, you may notice how mind and body interact to make an experience known, without the need to claim that process as self.

In a moment of seeing a blue color, tasting a salty flavor, or sensing a painful pressure—that is, in a moment of sensory contact—try to identify the functioning of each of the five aggregates. Know that they are conditioned processes of matter and mind—not a thing to identify with.

Once you can easily recognize each aggregate individually in ordinary sense contacts, then practice observing their interplay in daily experience at home, at work, while exercising, while shopping, and while sitting in formal meditation. Try to distinguish the unique functions of each aggregate, but also recognize that it is impossible to separate them—they usually arise and function together.

In this way, you can be mindful of the flow of changing sensory impressions as dynamic mind-body processes. When seeing them as conditioned processes, you are not investing in the story of self or fabricating a self-image that is based upon them.

the world. Not clinging, he is not agitated. Being unagitated, he personally attains Nibbāna."[95]

Whether you choose to structure your investigation with the five-aggregate model or the six-sense base model, or you elect to work with whatever is predominant in your present experience, highlighting clinging and its causes is the key to truly going beyond distraction and freeing the mind.

Clinging to Past, Present, and Future

Insight into the workings of thought can loosen the grip on personal tales of who we are, what we did, and what we will become. The Buddha taught his disciples in this way; he asked,

> Knowing and seeing in this way, would you run back to the past thus: "Were we in the past? Were we not in the past? What were we in the past? How were we in the past? Having been what, what did we become in the past?"
>
> And they replied, "No, venerable sir."
>
> Knowing and seeing in this way, would you run forward to the future thus: "Shall we be in the future? Shall we not be in the future? What shall we be in the future? How shall we be in the future? Having been what, what shall we become in the future?"
>
> "No, venerable sir."
>
> Knowing and seeing in this way, would you now be inwardly perplexed about the present thus: "Am I? Am I not? What am I? How am I? Where has this being come from? Where will it go?"
>
> "No, venerable sir."[96]

By thoroughly examining your lived experience, you will discover no independently existing entity called *self* in the past, in the future, or even in the present. By looking carefully, however, you can witness the habit of *commenting* on past, present, or future as a way to reinforce an illusory sense of self. You will learn how converting experiences into personal stories allows them to be clung to, and how clinging to a presumed position of self can sustain the corruptions of desire and aversion.

By gradually working through the coarsest defilements, you expose the subtler obstructive patterns that enable even minor defilements to control your mind. As you systematically work with distractions through this training, you effectively weaken all the fetters—notably the fetters of self-grasping, craving, conceit, delusion, and restlessness. Practice! Leave no obstacles that could thwart awakening.

Defilements can function only in conjunction with restlessness and delusion. If anger arises, it arises in conjunction with restlessness and delusion. If greed occurs, it occurs in conjunction with restlessness and delusion. Since defilements cannot function without restlessness and deluded misperceptions, a thorough practice of removing distraction will not only strengthen concentration, but can also be profoundly liberating.

Non-Identification with Attainments

As your spiritual practice develops, you may find that it becomes easy to let go. You might dwell for prolonged periods with a mind deliciously free from habitual distraction. You might experience profoundly concentrated and clear states, blissful absorptions and genuine glimpses of the empty nature of mind. You may have wondered in frustration why such spiritual perceptions don't last, why pesky distracting thoughts eventually return, why your concentration later fades, why you were not enlightened once and for all.

Even in the Buddha's time his disciples had many profound experiences, but sometimes their transformations didn't last, and they wondered what had gone wrong. In one discourse, a disciple describes his attainment of first jhāna. He notices, "I have gained the attainment of first jhāna." But soon after emerging from the absorption he feels pride in his accomplishment, exalts himself for

🌥 *Insight into the Mind That Is Having Insight*

Just as we contemplate perceptions of body, senses, and mind as impermanent, unsatisfactory, and not-self, we must also contemplate the mind that is perceiving the insight as impermanent, unsatisfactory, and not-self. The mind in the moment of insight must also be examined, contemplated, and seen to be ungraspable.

If we neglect to see the impermanence of an insight into impermanence, we might construct an enduring story around it. If we neglect to contemplate the unsatisfactory and ungraspable nature of mindfulness, we might turn direct insight into mere views and opinions about how things are. If we forget that even powerful direct realizations of emptiness are *also* empty of self, we might claim to be an enlightened one and seek recognition and status by boasting of our attainments.

So, continue to nurture mindful investigation. Observe the body, feelings, perceptions, and mind in the moment of having insight, and know that this experience of insight is also impermanent, unsatisfactory, and not-self.

that attainment, and disparages others who have not attained that level of concentration. And he does not progress.

Another disciple recalls a helpful instruction. "The Blessed One has spoken of non-identification (atammayatā) even with regard to the attainment of the first jhāna, for however they construe it to be, the truth is necessarily other than that."[97] So, by making non-identification his focal point, he neither exalts himself for his attainment of jhāna nor disparages others who have not developed concentration. And his practice progresses.

Similarly, non-identification is taught in regard to other spiritual accomplishments including all the concentrated jhāna states, formless spheres, and insight knowledges.

The human mind can distort any experience through comparison, identification, and possessiveness. Short of full enlightenment, meditators are vulnerable and can come under the sway of habitual thoughts that construct attachment. We must be wary of any tendency to conceive of a self as one who possesses experiences, to identify with attainments, and to judge "my" advantages or progress against that of another person.

We might have a nice experience in meditation and become delighted by it. Attached to that pleasure, we feel proud, seek recognition, show off a bit, and build a story that "I am really good at this meditation." We may hope that someone will see us sitting very still or imagine becoming a meditation teacher. To prevent the habit of identification from becoming a cause that corrupts spiritual attainments, base your practice upon a commitment to non-identification. Dispel any pride that might stagnate your potential. Remember not to take experiences personally—not even spiritual experiences!

ACHIEVING MASTERY

The strategies presented in this book offer ways to recognize your habitual tendencies, calm your mind, nurture both tranquility and wisdom through meditation, and allow these beneficial qualities to pervade your daily activities and interactions. Diligently abandoning habitual thoughts will gradually weaken defilements, enhance tranquility, and enable you to clearly see the dynamics of perception. Concentration is a critical element in a liberating meditation practice, but temporarily settling thoughts during meditation is not the end of the Buddhist path. By helping you to clearly see the underlying misperceptions that compel you to indulge habitual distractions, this training can empower you to discern when your experience is distorted by clinging and when it is free from clinging.

To develop liberating insight, we move beyond the simple wish to abandon repeatedly distracting thoughts or the desire to enjoy the beautiful stillness of concentration. We learn to skillfully apply attention so that we recognize the impermanence of all experiences and comprehend the liberating implication that, indeed, all aspects of conditioned experience are empty of self.

Throughout this practice, you have developed a supportive blend of concentration and insight by removing distractions, settling the mind, and contemplating the impermanent and empty condition of things. By replacing unskillful thoughts with more skillful alternatives (strategy #1), you know that you are not stuck—your thoughts, habits, and mental states are responsive to change; you can alter the inclination of your mind. By examining the danger (strategy #2), you recognize the harm caused by distorted perceptions, and become motivated to free your mind. By learning to withdraw attention (strategy #3), you intervene in the force of habit, pause, and free your energies for wiser pursuits. By investigating causes (strategy #4), you unravel how thoughts, feelings, and emotions produce the illusion of a self, distort perception, and inhibit liberating insights. By asserting your determination (strategy #5), you elevate your commitment to liberation over the tendency to indulge habits.

Systematically working with these strategies is a means to free your mind from the patterns that fuel defilements, from the distractions that obstruct your concentration, and from the distortions that obscure your ability to see things as they really are. As the habitual obstacles weaken, your mind becomes steadied and free to go beyond distraction and incline toward full and final liberation.

If this book has included more lists or steps than you care to remember, keep the practice simple. Clear your mind of habitual obsessions. Open to a fresh and free perspective on whatever is happening here and now. Don't take things personally. And practice not clinging to anything.

The Buddha offered some simple advice:

> Doing no evil,
> Engaging in what is skillful,
> And purifying one's mind:
> This is the teaching of the Buddhas.
> —Dhammapada 183[98]

SUMMARY OF MAIN POINTS

A mind free from distraction has the potential to experience states of deep concentration and liberating insights. Many habitual thoughts project a familiar self-image and keep the attention gripping a fictional construct—*the story of me*. When mindfulness, concentration, and wisdom are undeveloped, we misperceive sensory encounters, and the ensuing distorted thinking culminates in suffering. On the other hand, when supported by the stability of a concentrated mind and the continuity of mindfulness, sensory encounters will be known as merely impermanent perceptions, empty of self. Then, thoughts that might serve to fabricate self-constructs do not arise. This clear, mindful encounter with experience moves us beyond distraction, toward a liberating realization of the insubstantial and empty nature of things.

APPENDIX 1

DVEDHĀVITAKKA SUTTA: TWO KINDS OF THOUGHT[99]

1. Thus have I heard. On one occasion the Blessed One was living at Sāvatthī in Jeta's Grove, Anāthapiṇḍika's Park. There he addressed the bhikkhus thus: "Bhikkhus."—"Venerable sir," they replied. The Blessed One said this:

2. "Bhikkhus, before my enlightenment, while I was still only an unenlightened Bodhisatta, it occurred to me: 'Suppose that I divide my thoughts into two classes.' Then I set on one side thoughts of sensual desire, thoughts of ill will, and thoughts of cruelty, and I set on the other side thoughts of renunciation, thoughts of non–ill will, and thoughts of non-cruelty.

3. "As I abided thus, diligent, ardent, and resolute, a thought of sensual desire arose in me. I understood thus: 'This thought of sensual desire has arisen in me. This leads to my own affliction, to others' affliction, and to the affliction of both; it obstructs wisdom, causes difficulties, and leads away from Nibbāna.' When I considered: 'This leads to my own affliction,' it subsided in me; when I considered: 'This leads to others' affliction,' it subsided in me; when I considered: 'This leads to the affliction of both,' it subsided in me; when I considered: 'This obstructs wisdom, causes difficulties, and leads away from Nibbāna,' it subsided in me. Whenever a thought

of sensual desire arose in me, I abandoned it, removed it, did away with it.

4–5. "As I abided thus, diligent, ardent, and resolute, a thought of ill will arose in me . . . a thought of cruelty arose in me. I understood thus: 'This thought of cruelty has arisen in me. This leads to my own affliction, to others' affliction, and to the affliction of both; it obstructs wisdom, causes difficulties, and leads away from Nibbāna.' When I considered thus . . . it subsided in me. Whenever a thought of cruelty arose in me, I abandoned it, removed it, did away with it.

6. "Bhikkhus, whatever a bhikkhu frequently thinks and ponders upon, that will become the inclination of his mind. If he frequently thinks and ponders upon thoughts of sensual desire, he has abandoned the thought of renunciation to cultivate the thought of sensual desire, and then his mind inclines to thoughts of sensual desire. If he frequently thinks and ponders upon thoughts of ill will . . . upon thoughts of cruelty, he has abandoned the thought of non-cruelty to cultivate the thought of cruelty, and then his mind inclines to thoughts of cruelty.

7. "Just as in the last month of the rainy season, in the autumn, when the crops thicken, a cowherd would guard his cows by constantly tapping and poking them on this side and that with a stick to check and curb them. Why is that? Because he sees that he could be flogged, imprisoned, fined, or blamed [if he let them stray into the crops]. So too I saw in unwholesome states danger, degradation, and defilement, and in wholesome states the blessing of renunciation, the aspect of cleansing.

8. "As I abided thus, diligent, ardent, and resolute, a thought of renunciation arose in me. I understood thus: 'This thought of renunciation has arisen in me. This does not lead to my own affliction, or to others' affliction, or to the affliction of both; it aids wisdom, does not cause difficulties, and leads to Nibbāna. If I think and ponder upon this thought even for a night, even for a day, even

for a night and day, I see nothing to fear from it. But with excessive thinking and pondering I might tire my body, and when the body is tired, the mind becomes strained, and when the mind is strained, it is far from concentration.' So I steadied my mind internally, quieted it, brought it to singleness, and concentrated it. Why is that? So that my mind should not be strained.

9–10. "As I abided thus, diligent, ardent, and resolute, a thought of non–ill will arose in me . . . a thought of non-cruelty arose in me. I understood thus: 'This thought of non-cruelty has arisen in me. This does not lead to my own affliction, or to others' affliction, or to the affliction of both; it aids wisdom, does not cause difficulties, and leads to Nibbāna. If I think and ponder upon this thought even for a night, even for a day, even for a night and day, I see nothing to fear from it. But with excessive thinking and pondering I might tire my body, and when the body is tired, the mind becomes strained, and when the mind is strained, it is far from concentration.' So I steadied my mind internally, quieted it, brought it to singleness, and concentrated it. Why is that? So that my mind should not be strained.

11. "Bhikkhus, whatever a bhikkhu frequently thinks and ponders upon, that will become the inclination of his mind. If he frequently thinks and ponders upon thoughts of renunciation, he has abandoned the thought of sensual desire to cultivate the thought of renunciation, and then his mind inclines to thoughts of renunciation. If he frequently thinks and ponders upon thoughts of non–ill will . . . upon thoughts of non-cruelty, he has abandoned the thought of cruelty to cultivate the thought of non-cruelty, and then his mind inclines to thoughts of non-cruelty.

12. "Just as in the last month of the hot season, when all the crops have been brought inside the villages, a cowherd would guard his cows while staying at the root of a tree or out in the open, since he needs only to be mindful that the cows are there; so too, there was need for me only to be mindful that those states were there.

13. "Tireless energy was aroused in me and unremitting mindfulness was established, my body was tranquil and untroubled, my mind concentrated and unified.

14–23. "Quite secluded from sensual pleasures, secluded from unwholesome states, I entered upon and abided in the first jhāna . . . (*as in MN 4 Bhayabherava Sutta §§23–32*) . . . I directly knew: 'Birth is destroyed, the holy life has been lived, what had to be done has been done, there is no more coming to any state of being.'

24. "This was the third true knowledge attained by me in the last watch of the night. Ignorance was banished and true knowledge arose, darkness was banished and light arose, as happens in one who abides diligent, ardent, and resolute.

25. "Suppose, bhikkhus, that in a wooded range there was a great low-lying marsh near which a large herd of deer lived. Then a man appeared desiring their ruin, harm, and bondage, and he closed off the safe and good path to be traveled joyfully, and he opened up a false path, and he put out a decoy and set up a dummy so that the large herd of deer might later come upon calamity, disaster, and loss. But another man came desiring their good, welfare, and protection, and he reopened the safe and good path that led to their happiness, and he closed off the false path, and he removed the decoy and destroyed the dummy, so that the large herd of deer might later come to growth, increase, and fulfillment.

26. "Bhikkhus, I have given this simile in order to convey a meaning. This is the meaning: 'The great low-lying marsh' is a term for sensual pleasures. 'The large herd of deer' is a term for beings. 'The man desiring their ruin, harm, and bondage' is a term for Māra the Evil One. 'The false path' is a term for the wrong eightfold path, that is: wrong view, wrong intention, wrong speech, wrong action, wrong livelihood, wrong effort, wrong mindfulness, and wrong concentration. 'The decoy' is a term for delight and lust. 'The dummy' is a term for ignorance. 'The man desiring their good, welfare, and protection' is a term for the Tathāgata, accomplished and fully

enlightened. 'The safe and good path to be traveled joyfully' is a term for the Noble Eightfold Path, that is: right view, right intention, right speech, right action, right livelihood, right effort, right mindfulness, and right concentration.

"So, bhikkhus, the safe and good path to be traveled joyfully has been reopened by me, the wrong path has been closed off, the decoy removed, the dummy destroyed.

27. "What should be done for his disciples out of compassion by a teacher who seeks their welfare and has compassion for them, that I have done for you, bhikkhus. There are these roots of trees, these empty huts. Meditate, bhikkhus, do not delay or else you will regret it later. This is our instruction to you."

That is what the Blessed One said. The bhikkhus were satisfied and delighted in the Blessed One's words.

APPENDIX 2

VITAKKASAṆṬHĀNA SUTTA: THE REMOVAL OF DISTRACTING THOUGHTS[100]

1. Thus have I heard. On one occasion the Blessed One was living at Sāvatthī in Jeta's Grove, Anāthapiṇḍika's Park. There he addressed the bhikkhus thus: "Bhikkhus."—"Venerable sir," they replied. The Blessed One said this:

2. "Bhikkhus, when a bhikkhu is pursuing the higher mind, from time to time he should give attention to five signs. What are the five?

3. (i) "Here, bhikkhus, when a bhikkhu is giving attention to some sign, and owing to that sign there arise in him evil unwholesome thoughts connected with desire, with hate, and with delusion, then he should give attention to some other sign connected with what is wholesome. When he gives attention to some other sign connected with what is wholesome, then any evil unwholesome thoughts connected with desire, with hate, and with delusion are abandoned in him and subside. With the abandoning of them his mind becomes steadied internally, quieted, brought to singleness, and concentrated. Just as a skilled carpenter or his apprentice might knock out, remove, and extract a coarse peg by means of a fine one, so too . . . when a bhikkhu gives attention to some other sign connected with what is wholesome . . . his mind

becomes steadied internally, quieted, brought to singleness, and concentrated.

4. (ii) "If, while he is giving attention to some other sign connected with what is wholesome, there still arise in him evil unwholesome thoughts connected with desire, with hate, and with delusion, then he should examine the danger in those thoughts thus: 'These thoughts are unwholesome, they are reprehensible, they result in suffering.' When he examines the danger in those thoughts, then any evil unwholesome thoughts connected with desire, with hate, and with delusion are abandoned in him and subside. With the abandoning of them his mind becomes steadied internally, quieted, brought to singleness, and concentrated. Just as a man or a woman, young, youthful, and fond of ornaments, would be horrified, humiliated, and disgusted if the carcass of a snake or a dog or a human being were hung around his or her neck, so too . . . when a bhikkhu examines the danger in those thoughts . . . his mind becomes steadied internally, quieted, brought to singleness, and concentrated.

5. (iii) "If, while he is examining the danger in those thoughts, there still arise in him evil unwholesome thoughts connected with desire, with hate, and with delusion, then he should try to forget those thoughts and should not give attention to them. When he tries to forget those thoughts and does not give attention to them, then any evil unwholesome thoughts connected with desire, with hate, and with delusion are abandoned in him and subside. With the abandoning of them his mind becomes steadied internally, quieted, brought to singleness, and concentrated. Just as a man with good eyes who did not want to see forms that had come within range of sight would either shut his eyes or look away, so too . . . when a bhikkhu tries to forget those thoughts and does not give attention to them . . . his mind becomes steadied internally, quieted, brought to singleness, and concentrated.

6. (iv) "If, while he is trying to forget those thoughts and is not

giving attention to them, there still arise in him evil unwholesome thoughts connected with desire, with hate, and with delusion, then he should give attention to stilling the thought-formation of those thoughts. When he gives attention to stilling the thought-formation of those thoughts, then any evil unwholesome thoughts connected with desire, with hate, and with delusion are abandoned in him and subside. With the abandoning of them his mind becomes steadied internally, quieted, brought to singleness, and concentrated. Just as a man walking fast might consider: 'Why am I walking fast? What if I walk slowly?' and he would walk slowly; then he might consider: 'Why am I walking slowly? What if I stand?' and he would stand; then he might consider: 'Why am I standing? What if I sit?' and he would sit; then he might consider: 'Why am I sitting? What if I lie down?' and he would lie down. By doing so he would substitute for each grosser posture one that was subtler. So too . . . when a bhikkhu gives attention to stilling the thought-formation of those thoughts . . . his mind becomes steadied internally, quieted, brought to singleness, and concentrated.

7. (v) "If, while he is giving attention to stilling the thought-formation of those thoughts, there still arise in him evil unwholesome thoughts connected with desire, with hate, and with delusion, then, with his teeth clenched and his tongue pressed against the roof of his mouth, he should beat down, constrain, and crush mind with mind. When, with his teeth clenched and his tongue pressed against the roof of his mouth, he beats down, constrains, and crushes mind with mind, then any evil unwholesome thoughts connected with desire, with hate, and with delusion are abandoned in him and subside. With the abandoning of them his mind becomes steadied internally, quieted, brought to singleness, and concentrated. Just as a strong man might seize a weaker man by the head or shoulders and beat him down, constrain him, and crush him, so too . . . when, with his teeth clenched and his tongue pressed against the roof of his mouth, a bhikkhu beats down, constrains, and crushes mind with

mind . . . his mind becomes steadied internally, quieted, brought to singleness, and concentrated.

8. "Bhikkhus, when a bhikkhu is giving attention to some sign, and owing to that sign there arise in him evil unwholesome thoughts connected with desire, with hate, and with delusion, then when he gives attention to some other sign connected with what is wholesome, any such evil unwholesome thoughts are abandoned in him and subside, and with the abandoning of them his mind becomes steadied internally, quieted, brought to singleness, and concentrated. When he examines the danger in those thoughts . . . When he tries to forget those thoughts and does not give attention to them . . . When he gives attention to stilling the thought-formation of those thoughts . . . When, with his teeth clenched and his tongue pressed against the roof of his mouth, he beats down, constrains, and crushes mind with mind, any such evil unwholesome thoughts are abandoned in him . . . and his mind becomes steadied internally, quieted, brought to singleness, and concentrated. This bhikkhu is then called a master of the courses of thought. He will think whatever thought he wishes to think and he will not think any thought that he does not wish to think. He has severed craving, flung off the fetters, and with the complete penetration of conceit he has made an end of suffering."

That is what the Blessed One said. The bhikkhus were satisfied and delighted in the Blessed One's words.

ACKNOWLEDGMENTS

THIS BOOK DEVELOPED as a collaborative project with several friends and dedicated students. I am grateful for their contribution of ideas and real-life examples that brought this material to life. In particular, I thank Adhimutti Bhikkhuni, Amy D'Andrade, Anālayo Bhikkhu, Deborah Ventura, Dorothy Rogers, Ed Haertel, Greg Dalziel, Jackie Hutto, Maryleigh Burke, Olivia Vaz, Phil Jones, Robin Boudette, Robin Velasco, Steve Gasner, and Terry Farrah for their creative suggestions, editing assistance, and critical input.

I am especially grateful for Bhikkhu Ñaṇamoli and Bhikkhu Bodhi, who translated the discourses of the Buddha that inspired this book, and Wisdom Publications for generously including these translations in my appendices.

It has been a joy to work with the wonderful team at Wisdom Publications. Their enthusiasm for the theme of distraction and their skills in editing, design, and publication shaped this book.

My family, Elizabeth, Lisa, and Philip are an ongoing source of support for my life and work. My love and appreciation for them is beyond words!

SHAILA CATHERINE
San Jose, California

LIST OF ABBREVIATIONS

AN Aṅguttara Nikāya, the Numerical Discourses of the Buddha
Dhp Dhammapada
DN Dīgha Nikāya, the Long Discourses of the Buddha
MN Majjhima Nikāya, the Middle Length Discourses of the Buddha
SN Saṃyutta Nikāya, the Connected Discourses of the Buddha
Ud Udāna, the Inspired Utterances of the Buddha

CITATIONS

The key below will assist readers in deciphering my presentation of citations in the endnotes. I have relied upon the English-language translations listed in the bibliography and have not consulted texts written in the Pāli language. I follow the numbering system used by Bhikkhu Bodhi and other contemporary English translators, not the Pāli Text Society's conventional numbering system.

Aṅguttara Nikāya: AN is followed by a number that represents the collection (chapter), then a colon, then a number that designates the discourse within that collection (chapter), and finally, when available, the English name of the discourse.

Dhammapada: Dhp is followed by a number indicating the verse numbered from beginning of the Dhammapada.

Dīgha Nikāya: DN is followed by the number of the discourse as it appears within DN, followed by a period, then a number indicating the verse within the designated sutta, and finally the Pāli name of the discourse.

Majjhima Nikāya: MN is followed by a the number of the discourse as it appears within MN, followed by a period, then a number indicating the verse within that designated sutta, then the Pāli name of the discourse, and finally the English translation of the name of the discourse.

Saṃyutta Nikāya: SN is followed by a number that represents the collection (chapter or *saṃyutta*), followed by a colon, then a number that designates the discourse within that collection (also called chapter or saṃyutta), then the Pāli name of collection (again called saṃyutta), and finally, when available, the English name of the discourse.

The Udāna: Ud is followed by a number that indicates the chapter, followed by a colon, then a number that designates the discourse within that chapter, and finally, when available, the English name of the discourse.

NOTES

INTRODUCTION

1. AN 1:39–40. Bodhi trans. 2012.
2. AN 1:48. Bodhi trans. 2012.
3. SN 9:11 Vanasaṃyutta, Unwholesome Thoughts. Bodhi 2000.
4. AN 3:102 A Goldsmith. Bodhi trans. 2012.
5. MN 19 Dvedhāvitakka Sutta: Two Kinds of Thought and MN 20 Vitakkasaṇṭhāna Sutta: The Removal of Distracting Thoughts. Ñāṇamoli trans. 1995. I have chosen to use the rendering of the title, *The Removal of Distracting Thoughts*, as found in Ñāṇamoli and Bodhi's translation. A more literal translation of the title might be "Discourse on Stilling Thoughts."

CHAPTER 1. KNOWING YOUR OWN MIND

6. SN 47:35 Satipaṭṭhānasaṃyutta, Mindful. Bodhi trans. 2000.
7. Brewer, Garrison, Whitfield-Gabrieli 2013.
8. Goleman and Davidson 2017, 150–59.
9. AN 6:44 Migasālā. Bodhi trans. 2012.

CHAPTER 2. THOUGHTS THAT HELP AND THOUGHTS THAT HURT

10. MN 19.6 Dvedhāvitakka Sutta, Two Kinds of Thought. Ñāṇamoli trans. 1995.
11. MN 19 Dvedhāvitakka Sutta, Two Kinds of Thought. Ñāṇamoli trans. 1995.
12. Killingsworth and Gilbert 2010.
13. MN 89.12 Dhammacetiya Sutta, Monuments to the Dhamma. Ñāṇamoli trans. 1995.
14. SN 35:130 Saḷāyatanasaṃyutta, Hāliddakāni. Bodhi trans. 2000.

15. SN 36:19 Vedanāsaṃyutta, Pañcakaṅga. Bodhi trans. 2000.
16. MN 19.3 Dvedhāvitakka Sutta, Two Kinds of Thought. Ñāṇamoli trans. 1995.
17. MN 19.6 Dvedhāvitakka Sutta, Two Kinds of Thought. Ñāṇamoli trans. 1995.
18. MN 19.9 Dvedhāvitakka Sutta, Two Kinds of Thought. Ñāṇamoli trans. 1995.
19. MN 19.12 Dvedhāvitakka Sutta, Two Kinds of Thought. Ñāṇamoli trans. 1995.
20. Brewer, Davis, Goldstein 2013. 4:75–80.
21. Brewer 2017.
22. MN 21.8 Kakacūpama Sutta, The Simile of the Saw. Ñāṇamoli trans. 1995.
23. MN 19.8 Dvedhāvitakka Sutta, Two Kinds of Thought. Ñāṇamoli trans. 1995.

CHAPTER 3. ANTIDOTES AND ALTERNATIVES

24. MN 20.3 Vitakkasaṇṭhāna Sutta, The Removal of Distracting Thoughts. Ñāṇamoli trans. 1995.
25. MN 20 Vitakkasaṇṭhāna Sutta, The Removal of Distracting Thoughts. Ñāṇamoli trans. 1995.
26. MN 20.3 Vitakkasaṇṭhāna Sutta, The Removal of Distracting Thoughts. Ñāṇamoli trans. 1995.
27. MĀ 101 Anālayo and Bucknell trans. and eds. 2020.
28. McGonigal 2016.
29. McGonigal 2016.

CHAPTER 4. WEIGHING THE COSTS

30. MN 20.4 Vitakkasaṇṭhāna Sutta, The Removal of Distracting Thoughts. Ñāṇamoli trans. 1995.
31. MN 20.4 Vitakkasaṇṭhāna Sutta, The Removal of Distracting Thoughts. Ñāṇamoli trans. 1995.
32. MN 19.6 Dvedhāvitakka Sutta, Two Kinds of Thought. Ñāṇamoli trans. 1995.
33. SN 35:230 Saḷāyatanasaṃyutta, The Fisherman Simile. Bodhi trans. 2000.
34. SN 35:19 Saḷāyatanasaṃyutta, Delight (1). Bodhi trans. 2000
35. MN 75.10 Māgandiya Sutta, To Māgandiya. Ñāṇamoli trans. 1995.
36. MN 75.10 Māgandiya Sutta, To Māgandiya. Ñāṇamoli trans. 1995.
37. MN 13.7 Mahādukkhakkhandha Sutta, The Greater Discourse on the Mass of Suffering. Ñāṇamoli trans. 1995.

38. SN 36:6 Vedanā Saṃyutta, The Dart. Bodhi trans. 2000.
39. MN 10.32 Satipaṭṭhāna Sutta, The Foundations of Mindfulness. Ñāṇamoli trans. 1995.
40. MN 54.16 Potaliya Sutta, To Potaliya. Ñāṇamoli trans. 1995.
41. MN 13.10 Mahādukkhakkhandha Sutta, The Greater Discourse on the Mass of Suffering. Ñāṇamoli trans. 1995.
42. MN 13.12 Mahādukkhakkhandha Sutta, The Greater Discourse on the Mass of Suffering. Ñāṇamoli trans. 1995.
43. MN 13.14 Mahādukkhakkhandha Sutta, The Greater Discourse on the Mass of Suffering. Ñāṇamoli trans. 1995.
44. SN 35:13 Saḷāyatanasaṃyutta, Before My Enlightenment (1). Bodhi trans. 2000.
45. AN 5:41 Utilization. Bodhi trans. 2012.
46. AN 4:62 Freedom from Debt. Bodhi trans. 2012.
47. MN 13.16 Mahādukkhakkhandha Sutta, The Greater Discourse on the Mass of Suffering. Ñāṇamoli trans. 1995.
48. AN 4:28 Noble Lineages. Bodhi trans. 2012.
49. SN 12:52 Nidānasaṃyutta, Clinging. Bodhi trans. 2000.
50. SN 12:52 Nidānasaṃyutta, Clinging. Bodhi trans. 2000.

CHAPTER 5. WITHDRAWING THE FUEL

51. SN 35:134 Saḷāyatanasaṃyutta, At Devadaha. Bodhi trans. 2000.
52. DN 21:2.3 Sakkapañha Sutta. Walshe trans. 1995.
53. MN 20.5 Vitakkasaṇṭhāna Sutta, The Removal of Distracting Thoughts. Ñāṇamoli trans. 1995.
54. Mack and Rock 1998.
55. Simons and Chabris 1999. This study was first published in *Perception*. In this paragraph, I have included material from their subsequent book, Chabris and Simons 2010.
56. MN 8.13 Sallekha Sutta, Effacement. Ñāṇamoli trans. 1995.
57. MN 8.12 Sallekha Sutta, Effacement. Ñāṇamoli trans. 1995.
58. MN 8.14 Sallekha Sutta, Effacement. Ñāṇamoli trans. 1995.
59. MN 8.14 Sallekha Sutta, Effacement. Ñāṇamoli trans. 1995.
60. MN 2.19 Sabbāsava Sutta, All The Taints. Ñāṇamoli trans. 1995.
61. AN 5:161 Removing Resentment. Bodhi trans. 2012. The five ways of removing grudges or resentment included in this discourse are (1) develop loving-kindness, (2) develop compassion, (3) develop equanimity, (4) pay no attention, (5) reflect upon kamma and the results of action.
62. Healy 2013.
63. Zanon, Hutz, Reppold, Zanger 2016.
64. SN 47:10 Satipaṭṭhānasaṃyutta, The Bhikkhunis' Quarter. Bodhi trans. 2000.

65. Soma 1981.
66. Ud 4:1 Meghiya Sutta. Ireland trans. 1997.

CHAPTER 6. UNRAVELING THE CAUSES

67. AN 6:97 Benefits and AN 6:104 Without Identification. Bodhi trans. 2012.
68. Soma 1981.
69. MN 20.6 Vitakkasaṇṭhāna Sutta, The Removal of Distracting Thoughts. Ñāṇamoli trans. 1995.
70. I first learned the acronym of RAIN in the mid-1980s from a vipassana teacher named Michele McDonald during a silent insight meditation retreat. Over the decades it has become a staple in mindfulness courses and therapeutic contexts.
71. MN 128.16 Upakkilesa Sutta, Imperfections. Ñāṇamoli trans. 1995.
72. AN 10:51 One's Own Mind. Bodhi trans. 2012.
73. AN 10:51 One's Own Mind. Bodhi trans. 2012.
74. AN 10:51 One's Own Mind. Bodhi trans. 2012.
75. AN 10:51 One's Own Mind. Bodhi trans. 2012.
76. SN 35:99 Saḷāyatanasaṃyutta, Concentration. Bodhi trans. 2000.
77. MN 20.6 Vitakkasaṇṭhāna Sutta, The Removal of Distracting Thoughts. Ñāṇamoli trans. 1995.

CHAPTER 7. SAYING NO AND MEANING IT!

78. MN 20.7 Vitakkasaṇṭhāna Sutta, The Removal of Distracting Thoughts. Ñāṇamoli trans. 1995.
79. MN 20.7 Vitakkasaṇṭhāna Sutta, The Removal of Distracting Thoughts. Ñāṇamoli trans. 1995.
80. MN 20.7 Vitakkasaṇṭhāna Sutta, The Removal of Distracting Thoughts. Ñāṇamoli trans. 1995.
81. MN 20.7 Vitakkasaṇṭhāna Sutta, The Removal of Distracting Thoughts. Ñāṇamoli trans. 1995.
82. Ud 4:1 Meghiya Sutta. Ireland trans. 1997.
83. SN 46:31 Bojjhaṅgasaṃyutta, Wholesome. Bodhi trans. 2000.
84. AN 2:5 Nyanaponika Thera, B. Bodhi 1999. To reduce gender implications, I replaced the translator's use of the term "manly" with the term "human." The Pāli terms are *purisathāmena, purisavīriyena, purisaparakkamena.*
85. McGonigal 2012.

Chapter 8. Applying the Five Strategies

86. MN 32.9 Mahāgosinga Sutta, The Greater Discourse in Gosinga. Ñāṇamoli trans. 1995.
87. SN 49:1 Sammappadhānasaṃyutta, The River Ganges. Bodhi trans. 2000 and AN 4:275 Four Right Strivings. Bodhi trans. 2012.
88. AN 4:115 Deeds. Bodhi trans. 2012.
89. AN 3:65 Kālāma Sutta. Bodhi trans. 2012.
90. MN 20 Vitakkasaṇṭhāna Sutta, The Removal of Distracting Thoughts. Ñāṇamoli trans. 1995.

Chapter 9. Mastering Your Mind

91. MN 20.8 Vitakkasaṇṭhāna Sutta, The Removal of Distracting Thoughts. Ñāṇamoli trans. 1995.
92. SN 35:85 Saḷāyatanasaṃyutta, Empty Is the World. Bodhi trans. 2000.
93. MN 18.16 Madhupiṇḍina Sutta, The Honeyball. Ñāṇamoli trans. 1995.
94. SN 38:15 Jambukhādakasaṃyutta, Identity. Bodhi trans. 2000.
95. SN 35:234 Saḷāyatanasaṃyutta, Udāyī. Bodhi trans. 2000.
96. MN 38.23 Mahātaṇhāsankhaya Sutta, The Greater Discourse on the Destruction of Craving. Ñāṇamoli trans. 1995.
97. MN 113.21 Sappurisa Sutta, The True Man. Ñāṇamoli trans. 1995.
98. Dhp 183. Fronsdal 2005.

Appendix 1. Dvedhāvitakka Sutta

99. MN 19 Dvedhāvitakka Sutta: Two Kinds of Thought. Ñāṇamoli trans. 1995.

Appendix 2. Vitakkasaṇṭhāna Sutta

100. MN 20 Vitakkasaṇṭhāna Sutta: The Removal of Distracting Thoughts. Ñāṇamoli trans. 1995.

BIBLIOGRAPHY

Translations and Commentary on Buddhist Texts

Anālayo, Bhikkhu, and Roderick Bucknell, trans. and eds. 2020. *The Madhyama Āgama*, vol. 2. MĀ 101, MĀ 102. Moraga: BDK America.

Bodhi, Bhikkhu, trans. 2000. *The Connected Discourses of the Buddha: A Translation of the Saṃyutta Nikāya*. Boston: Wisdom Publications.

———. 2012. *The Numerical Discourses of the Buddha: A Translation of the Aṅguttara Nikāya*. Boston: Wisdom Publications.

Fronsdal, Gil, trans. 2005. *The Dhammapada: A New Translation of the Buddhist Classic*. Boston: Shambhala Publications.

Ireland, John D., trans. 1997. *The Udāna and the Itivuttaka: Inspired Utterances of the Buddha and the Buddha's Sayings*. Kandy, Sri Lanka: Buddhist Publication Society.

Ñāṇamoli, Bhikkhu, trans. 1995. *The Middle Length Discourses of the Buddha: A Translation of the Majjhima Nikāya*. Ed. and rev. by Bhikkhu Bodhi. Boston: Wisdom Publications.

Nyanaponika Thera and Bhikkhu Bodhi, trans. and eds. 1999. *Numerical Discourses of the Buddha: An Anthology of Suttas from the Aṅguttara Nikāya*. Walnut Creek: Alta Mira Press.

Soma Thera, trans. *The Removal of Distracting Thoughts*. Kandy, Sri Lanka: Buddhist Publication Society. *Wheel* no. 21. 1981. Translation of MN 20 with commentary and subcommentary.

Walshe, Maurice, trans. 1995. *The Long Discourses of the Buddha: A Translation of the Dīgha Nikāya*. Boston: Wisdom Publications.

Contemporary Research

Brewer, Judson. 2017. *The Craving Mind*. New Haven: Yale University Press.

Brewer, Judson, Jake Davis, and Joseph Goldstein. 2013. "Why Is It So Hard to Pay Attention, or Is It? Mindfulness, the Factors of Awakening and Reward-Based Learning." *Mindfulness* 4:75–80. https://doi.org/10.1007/s12671-012-0164-8.

Brewer, Judson, Kathleen Garrison, and Susan Whitfield-Gabrieli. October 2013. "What About the 'Self' Is Processed in the Posterior Cingulate Cortex?" *Frontiers in Human Neuroscience* 7.

Chabris, Christopher, and Daniel Simons. 2010. *The Invisible Gorilla: How Our Intuitions Deceive Us*. New York: Random House.

Goleman, Daniel, and Richard Davidson. 2017. *Altered Traits*. New York: Penguin Random House.

Healy, Melissa. "Can You Get PTSD from Watching Media Coverage of an Event? Maybe." *Los Angeles Times*. December 9, 2013. https://www.latimes.com/sciencenow/la-sci-media-coverage-trauma-stress-20131209-story.html. Accessed December 2020.

Killingsworth, Matthew, and Daniel Gilbert. 2010. "A Wandering Mind Is an Unhappy Mind." *Science*. November 12. https://doi.org/10.1126/science.1192439.

Mack, Arien, and Irvin Rock. 1998. *Inattentional Blindness*. Cambridge: MIT Press.

McGonigal, Kelly. 2016. *The Upside of Stress: Why Stress Is Good for You, and How to Get Good at It*. New York: Penguin.

———. 2012. *The Willpower Instinct: How Self-Control Works, Why It Matters, and What You Can Do to Get More of It.* New York: Penguin.

Simons, Daniel, and Christopher Chabris. 1999. "Gorillas in Our Midst: Sustained Inattentional Blindness for Dynamic Events." *Perception* 28, no. 9:1059–74. https://doi.org/10.1068/p281059.

Zanon, Cristian, Claudio Hutz, Caroline Reppold, and Markus Zanger. 2016. "Are Happier People Less Vulnerable to Rumination, Anxiety, and Post-Traumatic Stress? Evidence from a Large-Scale Disaster." *Psicologia: Reflexão e Crítica* 29(20). https://doi.org/10.1186/s41155-016-0038-4.

INDEX OF EXERCISES

GENERAL INDEX

A

abandonment
   craving and, 30–31, 93–94, 96, 163
   frequent thoughts and, 38
   as right effort, 169
   of unwholesome states, 3, 34, 41–43,
      45, 47, 55–56, 73–74, 107–8, 145,
      153–55, 168–70, 188–89
   See also letting go
absorption, 85, 186. *See also* jhāna;
   concentration
abstention, 104–5
acceptance, 51, 57, 114, 130, 132, 139, 171
accomplishment, 25, 81, 123, 186, 188
action
   agreeable, disagreeable, beneficial, or
      harmful, 170
   appropriate, 42, 93, 97, 107, 118–19,
      145–46
   of body, speech, mind, 29, 36, 81, 88,
      104, 144, 157
   as conditioning force, 130
   intention and, 44, 157
   See also virtue
addiction, 95–96, 160–61
Āgama, Madhyama, 54–55
aggregates, five, 182–84
akusala. *See* thought: wholesome and
   unwholesome

alternatives
   advance preparation of, 68
   to unwholesome thoughts, 48, 70–71,
      122, 180
   to view of self, 68–69
   See also antidotes; flexibility
analyzing, 15, 17, 22, 25. *See also* criticism; judgment
anatomical parts, viewing people as,
   62, 68
anger, 43, 58, 68, 70, 74, 81, 131, 133, 147,
   179
   antidotes to, 63–65, 166–69, 174
   behaviors that trigger, 64
   cost of, 83
   felt in body, 146
   if not winning, 136
   resistance to, 145–46
   self-concept sustained by, 185–86
   training sequence for, 166–69
annoyance, 50–51, 64, 101
anticipation, 75, 87, 91, 140, 144–45, 179
   dangers of, 75
   proactive measures and, 172
antidotes
   to habits, 55–58, 70, 141–42, 160
   to hindrances, 61–68, 174
   mindfulness as universal, 23, 55, 67–68
   See also alternatives; habit; hindrance

ABOUT THE AUTHOR

 SHAILA CATHERINE has been leading medi-
tation retreats worldwide since 1996, empha-
sizing deep concentration, jhāna, and the path
of liberating insight. Shaila is the founder of
Bodhi Courses, an online Dhamma classroom,
and Insight Meditation South Bay, a Buddhist
meditation center in Silicon Valley in California. She has practiced meditation since 1980,
studied with founders of Western insight meditation centers, and
accumulated more than nine years of silent retreat experience.
Shaila spent most of the 1990s practicing with eminent masters
in India, Thailand, and Nepal. From 2006 to 2014, she practiced
under the guidance of Pa-Auk Sayadaw and twice completed his rig-
orous training in jhāna and vipassanā. Shaila loves deep meditation
and appreciates a variety of approaches to exploring, developing,
and liberating the mind. Shaila is the author of *Focused and Fearless: A Meditator's Guide to States of Deep Joy, Calm, and Clarity* and
*Wisdom Wide and Deep: A Practical Handbook for Mastering Jhāna
and Vipassanā.*

SHAILA CATHERINE (www.shailacatherine.com)
Bodhi Courses (www.bodhicourses.org)
Insight Meditation South Bay (www.imsb.org)

WHAT TO READ NEXT
FROM WISDOM PUBLICATIONS

FOCUSED AND FEARLESS
A Meditator's Guide to States of Deep Joy, Calm, and Clarity
Shaila Catherine
Foreword by Pa-Auk Sayadaw

"Shaila Catherine represents a new generation of Dharma practitioner in the West."—Sharon Salzberg, author of *Lovingkindness*

MINDFULNESS, BLISS, AND BEYOND
A Meditator's Handbook
Ajahn Brahm
Foreword by Jack Kornfield

"Riveting, rollicking, and uncompromisingly real."
—Glenn Wallis, author of *Basic Teachings of the Buddha*

MINDFULNESS IN PLAIN ENGLISH
Bhante Gunaratana

"A classic—one of the very best English sources for authoritative explanations of mindfulness."
—Daniel Goleman, author of *Emotional Intelligence*

WISDOM WIDE AND DEEP
A Practical Handbook for Mastering Jhāna and Vipassanā
Shaila Catherine

"If you are interested in Dharma study, then Shaila's book belongs in your library."—Phillip Moffitt

About Wisdom Publications

Wisdom Publications is the leading publisher of classic and contemporary Buddhist books and practical works on mindfulness. To learn more about us or to explore our other books, please visit our website at wisdomexperience.org or contact us as the address below.

Wisdom Publications
199 Elm Street
Somerville, MA 02144 USA

We are a 501(c)(3) organization, and donations in support of our mission are tax deductible.